MW01279873

A JOURNEY INTO THE MIND

Hypnosis

A JOURNEY INTO THE MIND

Hypnosis

Anita Anderson-Evangelista

ARCO PUBLISHING, INC.
NEW YORK

Published by Arco Publishing, Inc.
219 Park Avenue South, New York, N.Y. 10003

Copyright © 1980 by Anita L. Anderson-Evangelista

All rights reserved. No part of this book may be reproduced, by any means, without permission in writing from the publisher, except by a reviewer who wishes to quote brief excerpts in connection with a review in a magazine or newspaper.

Library of Congress Cataloging in Publication Data

Anderson-Evangelista, Anita L
Hypnosis.

Bibliography: p. 229
Includes index.
1. Hypnotism—Therapeutic use. 2. Hypnotism.
I. Title.
RC495.A53 616.89′162 79-27817
ISBN 0–668–04908–1 (Cloth Edition)
ISBN 0–668–05134–5 (Paper Edition)

Printed in the United States of America

To
Nick Evangelista, my husband,
for his advice, support and criticism,
and for always being there.

Contents

Introduction

It is the intention of this book to provide the beginning or advanced hypnotist with a readable, usable guide to the intelligent application of hypnosis, and to the true potential of the mind.

Throughout it should become obvious that I favor a "common sense" approach to the practice of this art. Dogmatic concepts and rituals will be done away with because experience has shown me that hard rules can make the practice of hypnosis rigid and not as successful as it must be to survive in professional usage. The beginning hypnotist generally starts with formulas, but must eventually cast them aside to advance skillfully. In the decade-plus that I have been doing hypnosis, I have yet to find one "rule" that cannot be effectively broken with good results.

This volume provides an in-depth view of all facets of hypnosis. It incorporates diverse ideas and techniques, knowing that the individuality of the hypnotist is just as crucial a factor to success as the quirks of his subject. You will discover that hypnosis, though it has no specific definition agreed upon by all, produces consistently remarkable and repeatable results—and you will learn how to do it yourself!

I have purposely excluded from consideration any so-called tests of hypnotizability for this reason: my experience has shown that the willingness of an individual to be hypnotized is a function of not only innate characteristics, but also of the setting, attitude and personality of the hypnotist, the physical condition of the subject, the weather,—plus concurrent factors which, for time considerations alone, cannot be tested at each session. The hypnotist's personal awareness and observational skills on a one-to-one basis will go a great deal further than any predetermined testing procedures.

If you are now taking or intend to enroll in a course in hypnosis, you'll find this a convenient text which summarizes the divergent beliefs of various excellent hypnotists. If you are practicing hypnotism, you will have the benefit of work that has gone before, and you will see how others have dealt with the kind of situations and subjects you are facing. You can apply material at your own rate and frequency.

But no one can become a decent hypnotist solely by reading, however wonderful the material. It is the application of technique and theory that does it, and it is therefore essential that you spend time actually placing people in hypnosis, so that you learn from your experience. For your development, you might also consider being hypnotized several times—you'll appreciate it better from having been there!

Hypnosis
A JOURNEY INTO THE MIND

CHAPTER ONE

Magnetizer? Magician? A Historical Perspective

Historically, modern hypnosis can trace its roots back only as far as the mid 1700's, when Count Mesmer began his experiments with magnets. However, mind-altering disciplines similar to hypnosis are probably as old as civilization itself.

Egyptian art depicts brain surgery performed by trepanning, a removable triangular section cut into the skull bone to allow access to the brain. Cultural archeologists have little reason to believe that Egypt's medical system included anesthetic or sterile practices. Yet, this surgery and other procedures just as complicated and dangerous were apparently performed routinely. Although not much is actually recorded regarding the surgical technique, some form of pain elimination must have been used. If it was not chemical, as archeologists state, it must have been mental—probably a type of induced anesthesia. Whether ancient Egyptians actually practiced what we term hypnosis may never be known, but it is certain they used some system to affect the mind.

Certain American Indian tribes, notably the Hopi, developed skilled medical practices, including the use of herbs and medicinal plants. Again, where complex surgery was used, it was necessary to eliminate pain. If the "medicine man" had no herb to relieve severe pain, could an incantation to the gods have brought relief? History notes that it often did . . . but seldom describes the exact process. The skilled use of suggestion was part of the Indian medical art—and suggestion is the basis of hypnosis.

MESMER TO COUÉ

In the mid 1700's, a Father Hell, astrologer to the Austrian Court, read a technical paper prepared by the young Frenchman, Count Frederick Anton Mesmer (1734–1815). It described his tentative research into the magnetic effect of planetary bodies on humans. Father Hell subsequently sent Count Mesmer a packet of magnets to aid the young doctor in continuing his studies. Mesmer's work led him to believe that there was some innate power in magnetism that could act upon the human organism and effect disease cures. After "magnetizing" an elm tree, he would tie a distressed person to it until results were seen—usually overnight. With sufficient motivation, many things are possible. Mesmer's hold on the French upper classes was enormous; his cures and success rate were indisputable.

Mesmer theorized that a "universal fluid," an etheric substance, was essential to the process. One Royal Academy of Science member's report[1] stated that a great force acted upon and mastered the patient, and appeared to come from the "magnetizer," the person performing the procedure. This was probably one of the first wrong assumptions given as explanations for the success of magnetism and hypnotism, and is one that still persists. It implies that the magnetizer or hypnotist has some power which he calls to the patient's aid, an unfortunate fallacy responsible for much of the fear still surrounding hypnosis today.

Refining his technique, Mesmer developed a magnetic appliance, the Bacquet, consisting of a large metal tub partially filled with iron filings and bottles submerged in water. Metal rods extended from the bacquet, and the afflicted were to grasp these while gentle background music played. When the magnetizer, Mesmer or one of his students, entered he would pronounce that the patients "be healed!" At that point, the sufferer could be expected to experience anything from mild euphoria to extreme convulsions. When this state passed, usually in one to three hours, the illness or complaint passed with it. Not only evanescent symptoms, such as tension headache, but paralysis, infection, insanity, blindness, lameness, tumors and gout were cured. Several treatments may have been required in stubborn cases.

In 1784, Louis XVI appointed a committee to study Mesmer's treatment. By this time, several priests had joined the magnetizer's ranks, but the Vatican had condemned making the blind see and the lame walk as travesties of Biblical truth. Traditional medical men were denouncing Mesmer's considerable successes as the products of hoax and trickery. The committee appointed by Louis XVI arrived at a time when Mesmer was unavailable so they only saw the work carried out by students. Incidentally, one of the illustrious members of the committee was Benjamin Franklin, American ambassador to France and much respected for his viewpoints and outlook. After several days, the committee reported back to Louis: "Imagination is everything; magnetism is nothing . . ."[2]

Mesmer fell from grace with the establishment of that

time, but continued his work with magnets until his death, over twenty years later.

Perhaps those fateful words of the investigative committee hold more meaning than is at first apparent. Recent work with hypnotism in the treatment of various cancers show that imaginative, constructive thoughts actually do affect cell growth and destruction. This is covered more fully later in the book. If magnetism, magnets and elm trees did not of themselves produce cures in the sick, could it have been the inner, imaginative mind of the patient that did?

About the time Louis' committee was investigating Mesmer, one of his prize students, the Marquis de Puységur (1751–1825), was making a unique discovery. He had magnetized a young, mentally retarded boy named Victor by exposing the youth to a magnetic elm. Under that influence, Victor developed a secondary personality: he could diagnose illness, his own and that of others even though miles away, and spoke with such authority on subjects like politics and religion that Puységur called his state "clairvoyance," or clear-seeing. The Marquis became something of a local joke when he insisted on calling the boy, "my intelligence."

Clairvoyance, of course, is one of the terms we now apply to extrasensory perception (ESP), which can range from medical diagnosis to an awareness of the thoughts and actions of others. The skills which Victor developed while magnetized correspond remarkably to the talents demonstrated by a modern psychic and mystic, Edgar Cayce (1877–1945)[3], who performed his feats while in a self-induced hypnotic state. The Marquis was to term this unusual condition "magnetic somnambulism," or magnetic sleepwalking. He continued his work without charge after Mesmer's death.

For a time magnetism went underground and was carried on primarily by stage entertainers. In the 1830's there was a popular mania for magnetism in Paris. French novelist Alexander Dumas, author of *The Three Musketeers*, believed himself to be an adept. In one experiment, a subject made numerous political prophecies—none of which were ever fulfilled!

In 1839, James Braid, a British M.D., watched a stage performance of magnetism and concluded that the entire demonstration was a hoax. He returned for three more shows, picking up a little more of the magnetizer's technique each time. He noticed that having the subject's eyes open or closed seemed to make a considerable difference in the success of the magnetism. Afterwards, he promptly magnetized his wife and two servants by having them stare at various common objects.

Braid was a clever and resourceful man. After several years of experiments he concluded that staring paralyzed the nerve centers of the eyes and destroyed the balance of the nervous system, thereby producing "sleep" as the magnetizer had. He basically demonstrated that it was not the "power" of the magnetizer that produced the state, but something within the subject. He called this condition "hypnosis," from the Greek *hypnos*, meaning sleep. He published his findings himself and they immediately brought him both great scorn and admiration. He later attempted to change "hypnotism" to "monoideism," i.e., one idea, but the first term had already caught on.

Aside from giving hypnosis its name, Braid is best known for his efforts to standardize induction techniques.[4] The body of his work became the basis of hypnotism for nearly a century.

About 1850, a Scottish surgeon practicing in India, James Esdaile, M.D. (1808–1859), read a few articles on the new science of hypnotism and on magnetism. He discovered he could induce a deep "sleep" by making specific hand passes over the patient's body. Using this system, he performed over 2,000 surgeries, 300 of them major operations—with only an 8 per cent mortality rate. Compare that to today's only slightly improved 5 per cent rate . . . and Esdaile worked without anesthesia, antibiotics or antiseptic practices! He later returned to England and attempted to set up a hypnotic practice with Dr. John Elliotson, another magnetizer. Although the system worked for a number of years, their hypnotic methods were difficult to duplicate. They were denounced as charlatans and their hospital was closed.

The Esdaile state is sometimes wrongly called the hypnotic "coma." Signs of this "coma" condition include total automatic anesthesia without suggestion, catatonia (the subject remains in whatever position he is placed), complete immobilization, no response to the hypnotist's suggestions (sometimes including the suggestion to awaken) and apparent loss of consciousness.

Though the subject does show these signs, he is, in fact, *not* in a coma. The subject, like anyone under hypnosis, retains an awareness of everything about him—including the hypnotist's efforts to awaken him. People who have experienced this state call it blissful, almost euphoric.[5]

France continued to lead the world in producing magnetizers and hypnotists well into the 1800's. In the 1890's a "Great Debate" began between France's three major schools of magnetism/hypnotism: those at Salpêtrière, at Nancy and the School of Charity.

The Salpêtrière school housed a number of authorities in various fields. The resident magnetizer was Jean-Martin Charcot (1825–1893), an M.D. with a practice consisting primarily of hysterical[6] women. Like Braid, he began using magnetism after viewing a stage performance. He discovered that the application of certain metals could influence the nerves and reflexes. A piece of copper, for example, might be placed on the back of the patient's neck to soothe and relax him. In fact, Charcot's research indicated that one patient's symptoms could be transferred to another via magnets!

It came as a great surprise to Charcot that some patients could recall what transpired while they were under magnetic influence. He determined that the effectiveness of the magnetic work was seldom hindered by whether the patient remembered or not. He called the state where memory loss was complete "grand hypnotisme," or deep sleep, and the state where some memory was retained "petit hypnotisme," or light sleep. Note that the descriptive words in Charcot's definitions are also applied to epileptic seisures—"grand mal" and "petit mal," translation of which is "very bad" and "a little bad" respectively.

In competition with Charcot and his Salpêtrière pupils was Dr. Luys at the School of Charity, who advocated the use of physical agents. Luys found that the appropriate medication in a small vial, when placed near a patient, could produce the same effect as having the patient actually ingest it. Furthermore, colored glass balls put in a patient's hand resulted in emotions corresponding to the color involved. Luys' procedures, however, invited criticism from all sides.

The final advocate in the "Great Debate" was the School at Nancy. Dr. Ambrose-August Liebeault (1823–1904), a country doctor, began his study of the new science of hypnotism after reading a report on hypnotic anesthesia. As early as 1866 he had worked with cases of rheumatism, epilepsy, neuralgia and paralysis, as well as published a book, *Concerning Sleep and Analogous States Considered in Particular from the Point of View of the Action of the State of Mind on the Physical State*. It sold exactly one copy. His colleagues regarded him as a quack. Hippolyte Bernheim (1837–1919), a professor from the Nancy School, was sent to expose him. However, Bernheim was so impressed by Liebeault's work that he was converted and began practicing hypnosis at Nancy. At his invitation Liebeault settled in Nancy. Their combined work eventually incorporated psychology and verbal suggestion, essentially the system used today.

The "Great Debate" came to an end with the passing of two events: the discrediting of Luys and the Charity School (Luys' experiments having been conducted so carelessly as to render them of no practical value) and Charcot's death in 1893, with the subsequent disbanding of his followers. The Nancy School remained, victorious as much by default as by its merits.

It was the Nancy technique of verbal suggestion which Sigmund Freud and his young student associates practiced. In the days prior to Freud's development of his theories of personality, he used hypnotism extensively in dream interpretation and the treatment of neuroses. Later, while performing a private experiment, he came to feel that the hypnotist left himself open to personal attachment by the subject—a circumstance which he believed would render hypnotism virtually useless. He therefore discontinued using hypnotism in his practice. Freud's subjects, however, continued to form attachments—a point Freud may not have seriously noted. It was not the act of hypnotizing a patient that caused "transference," as it came to be known, but the patient's emotional state and progress. Had Freud continued to use hypnosis, it undoubtedly would be a part of psychoanalysis today.[7]

In 1891, George du Maurier's novel *Trilby* caught an

unprepared world by surprise. It was the story of the evil Svengali using hypnotism to subvert a young woman's mind and will. To the unsuspecting public, hypnotism became the ultimate weapon: in the wrong hands, it could destroy the world! To date, hypnotism has yet to live down the misconceptions wrought by *Trilby*. The name "Svengali" has come to denote the archetypical hypnotist, the tall, thin man with dark, piercing eyes and pointed beard who can *make* people do things. Today's clients still say, "Make me stop smoking," as if the hypnotist had the power to activate people's will. The movie version of *Trilby* was remade five times—in 1914, 1917, 1923, 1932 and in 1953—and the story continues to affect modern audiences as strongly as the book did in its time.

By the 1920's, with the major portion of the Western Hemisphere enjoying unprecedented wealth, a new approach to selfhood was developing. Spearheading the self-improvement movement was Emil Coué, a Frenchman who toured the world with his new "auto-suggestion"[8] technique. Coué believed that each individual could condition or program himself through daily repetition. He spoke to massive audiences, gaining the reputation of a positive, self-possessed man. His ideas were rapidly incorporated into almost every personal achievement course—including the famous, "Everyday in every way, I get better and better."

Modern Times

Between the 1920's and 1950's hypnotism was largely a theatrical phenomena, although some individuals did find there was an application to more "serious" work. In 1951, Bernard Gindes, M.D., wrote a guideline to hypnotism, his *New Concepts of Hypnosis*. Gindes was in his mid-twenties at the time and just out of medical school. He demonstrated how very effective hypnosis could be in the analysis and treatment of physical symptoms. By 1976 he was to say about the book, "Anyone could write that today—it's common knowledge."[9] But in the 1950's it was all new and much needed.

By the late 1950's another book had caused public outcry and uproar. This one proposed no theories, nor created a new monster Svengali. It was Morey Bernstein's *The Search for Bridey Murphey*, a simple record of a woman's age regression into a past life.[10] Repercussions were of astounding proportions. National magazines carried rebuttals, the clergy denounced it from pulpits, editors received thousands of letters. Bernstein had made the unforgivable error of being a subjective observer of his subject's reactions. She spoke with an Irish brogue, used a vocabulary consistent with the past, even danced a jig. Bernstein also happened to have no degrees or "professional" hypnosis experience; he was simply an interested amateur. While medical and psychological scorn for his work grew, quiet "amateurs" began their own age regression tests.

Two names emerged from the 1960's as highly influential in hypnosis literature. William Kroeger, M.D., prepared his *Clinical and Experimental Hypnosis*, a technical volume designed to aid medical personnel. Written in such a manner as to be accessible to all interested readers, Kroeger's effort reflects the typical approach of the times: word your suggestion properly, repeat it, give proper encouragement and your patient must see some beneficial results. Leslie LeCron, however, appealed to both the professional and amateur hypnotist, and made a special approach to self-help enthusiasts with his *Self-Hypnotism*. One hypnotist has said, "LeCron wrote more books each year than I had time to read!"[11]

Out of the 1960's into the 1970's, two more individuals contributed divergent yet equally plausible explanations and theories of hypnosis. One of these is Milton Erickson, M.D., who overcame polio and colorblindness to introduce an indirect technique of hypnosis uniquely his own. His use of well-timed pauses, metaphors and similes is something of a contradiction of previously accepted technique. Erickson insists that existence of the "unconscious" mind is a literal fact which most other hypnotists ignore. Theodore X. Barber, Ph.D., on the other hand, states that there is in fact no unique, separate hypnotic state, and that the mind can accomplish the same effects as hypnotism without formal or informal induction. Task motivation becomes the most important factor, according to Barber, not the method of presentation. Both Erickson and Barber, however, each have impressive records and a body of research to confirm their findings.

In the Public View

Public opinion continues to play a major role in the acceptance and feasibility of hypnotic procedures. Although dentists, doctors and psychologists may favor specific, diagramatically provable approaches to the art, it is the general beliefs which make their work effective or not.

Movies, radio and television have made hypnotism a much-used plot device, comparable to the cavalry coming just in time, but in reverse. If the heroine does something unexpectedly bizarre, perhaps it is because she has been hypnotized against her will.

Orson Welles played the fanatic Caliostro in the movie *Black Magic*, which was based on Alexander Dumas' *Joseph Balsamo*. Caliostro, an intense dark man with piercing eyes, uses his wicked art to control a kingdom. Then, in *Abbott and Costello Meet the Killer*, Boris Karloff brought an "actual" hypnotic induction to the screen: turbaned Karloff mesmerizes innocent Costello using snaky hand passes. In the *Frozen Ghost*, Lon Chaney accidentally instructs one of his hypnotized subjects to die, and feels very guilty about it. *The Hypnotic Eye*—which had a genuine hypnotist as adviser, Gil Boyne[12]—depicted a crazed stage hypnotist who causes pretty women to mutilate themselves. In *Exorcist Two*, current research was innocently parodied in an utterly fanciful mutual hypnosis via biofeedback.[13] But the true horrors of the hypnotic monster were presented in *Telefon*, where unsuspecting people were forced to kill through hypnosis.

Similarly, several modern novels have continued the myth of the all-powerful hypnotist. Felice Picano's *The Mesmerist* recounts how a nineteenth century hypnotist seduces an entire town. *The Holland Suggestions* by John Dunning has the hero responding to suggestion twenty years after the fact, and *Links* by Charles Panati depicts an experiment in mutual hypnosis carried to extremes.

Two other examples—shining by comparison—tend to portray hypnosis somewhat more realistically. In *The Exorcist*, a brief scene with the possessed little girl and a psychologist-hypnotist portrays the possibility of the hypnotist also being human: the devil painfully grabs his genitals! *Audrey Rose* climaxes with a smug but inept psychologist-hypnotist doing more harm than good.

So, the average moviegoer/reader/TV watcher has a choice of two, not-quite-true extremes: the hypnotist as self-righteous clod, or the hypnotist as unscrupulous pow-ermonger. These misunderstandings are not limited to the "average" populace, either. Too often, I have had to re-assure a doctor—who should know better—that hypnosis will not rob him of his will power. Or a psychologist who fears that hypnosis will unleash subconscious monsters in his patients. Or a minister or priest who wonders if hyp-notism opens his flock to possession by evil spirits. It's obvious that the only contact such professionals have had with hypnosis has been through rumor and hearsay—and the entertainment industry.

The Traditional Approach and Variations

Nearly all schools of hypnosis agree on one basic con-sideration, and that is the Progressive or Fractional Relax-ation form of inducing hypnosis. It had its roots somewhere in Braid's work, then was carried on and elaborated by the Nancy school and formalized in this century. It appears not only in hypnosis, but in many other guises, as you'll see.

The Progressive Relaxation (PR) Induction centers, as the name implies, around muscular relaxation and subse-quent dissociation from external stimuli. Once the subject can focus his attention sufficiently to willfully produce re-laxation of major muscle groups, he is generally on the threshold of hypnosis. Very specific signs will indicate if this has occurred, and how much more guidance will be necessary to produce a functional state of hypnosis.

In some systems, rather than simply ask or suggest that the subject relax various muscles, he is told to tense specific muscles for several seconds, then relax them. The advan-tage here is that the subject can definitely tell when the muscles are relaxing, and has an opposite effect—tension—to play against. The PR induction is covered in Chapter Four.

The word "hypnosis" itself has gained, as we have seen, an unjustified and unsavory reputation over the years. Suppose an intelligent person wished to use the best of hypnotic technique without alarming his clients. He might simply rename it est or Silva or Dianetics, and sternly state that no wicked hypnotism whatsoever was involved. His clients would be put at ease, could respond freely to the "new" system, and gain the benefits of successful hypnosis.

With each new use of hypnotism small personal variations inevitably result, but the primary difference is in the *intent* of the school of thought. This is aptly demonstrated by the various ways the PR induction is currently used. It is interesting to note that each of the following disavows any use of hypnotism in any form:

Guided imagery or dreaming: used by psychologists and psychiatrists to elicit symbolic subconscious material from their patients. An undisguised PR induction proceeds all work, beginning with, "Close your eyes and take a deep breath . . ."

est: a partially sadistic system designed to demonstrate limitless personal potential. In addition to the PR form, est uses other hypnotic phenomena, including "creation" of mental work and rest areas and release of repressed material.

Silva Mind Control and its spin-offs: a mild program to encourage extrasensory perception skills. Again the PR form with a slight variation—a finger cue to reactivate or restimulate the state of hypnosis once it is achieved. Like est, it includes the creation of mental work areas, but with an emphasis on curing illness and helping others.

Dianetics: "religious" way of probing and releasing repressed memories. Uses a shortened version of the PR form, using counting and direct regression suggestions coupled with simple biofeedback.

TM and various meditative disciplines: used to promote inner balance and oneness with the universe. Several variations of the PR form, many with focus on breathing or repetitious sound such as ticking clock or heartbeat. Very little direct suggestion is used here, however.

Biofeedback: an objective method of teaching the patient to be aware of autonomous physical systems, such as heartbeat or blood pressure, to increase health. Various direct and indirect PR forms using teacher's voice, buzzing sound, visual displays, etc.

So, the unwary client submits himself to hypnosis nevertheless, and the benefits he receives are chalked up to the philosophy or system from which it came. It's important to remember that each of the above disciplines, and many others not mentioned, are popular and viable only because they *do* work. Generally, someone who has been through est or meditation, for example, will also be very amenable to hypnotic suggestion—because they have already experienced it! If individual salvation then, becomes a matter not of Dianetics or Silva, but instead of reaching that inner level of mind—by whatever name—perhaps the mind's intent is more important than the system.

The mental intent and beliefs that go with it are central to the next chapter.

Notes to Chapter One

1 *Powers of Hypnosis* by Dauvan (Stein and Day, 1969)
2 *Mesmer: Between God and Devil* by James Wyckoff (Prentice-Hall, 1975).
3 Edgar Cayce's work and a great body of literature devoted to his talents are available through the Association for Research and Enlightenment, Virginia Beach, Virginia.
4 Braid was one of the first to suggest relaxation and eye closure.
5 Dave Elman, author of *Explorations in Hypnosis* (Nash, 1967), has written that his research indicates that subjects thoroughly enjoy the "coma" state, and frequently comment that they were so comfortable their position didn't matter. The "coma" brings a complete and total euphoria. The subject, rather than allow himself to be disturbed, disregards any pain impulse, thereby producing anesthesia. Theory states that one in fifteen thousand people can achieve the "coma," but Elman insists—as Esdaile did—that the "coma" can be produced in anyone who can be hypnotized.
6 "Hysteria" derives from the root word *yster*, meaning womb. Hence we have "hysterectomy" for removal of the womb. Female reproductive organs were thought to be the root of hysteria!
7 In *Freud and Hypnosis*, by Milton Kline, Ph.D. (Agora Softback, Julian Press, 1966), the author unequivocably states that because of the legend surrounding Freud and his theories, Freud's view of hypnosis as obstructionist has come to be the basis of its rejection from serious consideration. Dr. Kline considers this treatment of hypnosis as one of the great scientific errors of modern times.
8 "Auto-suggestion" being a synonym for self-hypnosis.
9 Gindes made this remark to me during a meeting of the California Professional Hypnotist Association at which he was a guest speaker. He died in 1978.

10 I was fortunate to meet Bridey Murphey's alter ego, Virginia Tige, during the making of the movie *Audrey Rose*. I was startled at how utterly normal and un-Irish she was!

11 Said by William Deanyer, stage hypnotist, who owns a library of rare and unique hypnosis books. LeCron died in 1977.

12 Boyne doesn't mention this film often.

13 M.D. William Bauman and hypnotist Henry Prokop acted as technical advisors here. Prokop later suggested that the rigors of reality were less important to the filmmakers than emotional impact.

CHAPTER TWO

Relating to the World

In recent years, the living brain has been analyzed and probed down to the cellular level. It holds very few physical secrets from us. The thinking mind, however, remains largely unknown: how a thought develops, "where" it comes from, why some people's thoughts promote well-being and other's do not.

There may exist an actual system of Laws of Mental Function of which our science is as yet unaware—and perhaps they are just as substantial as the physical laws. Hypnosis, which delves into the deeper recesses of the mind, may be able to determine some of them. To do this, we must assess our current understanding of the mind.

Left Brain, Right Brain

The physical brain is a greyish organ encased within the skull. It consists of two halves, or hemispheres, separated by a longitudinal fissure and joined by a broad transverse of nerve fibers, the corpus callosum. Each hemisphere is about the size of a clenched fist, and has a series of creases

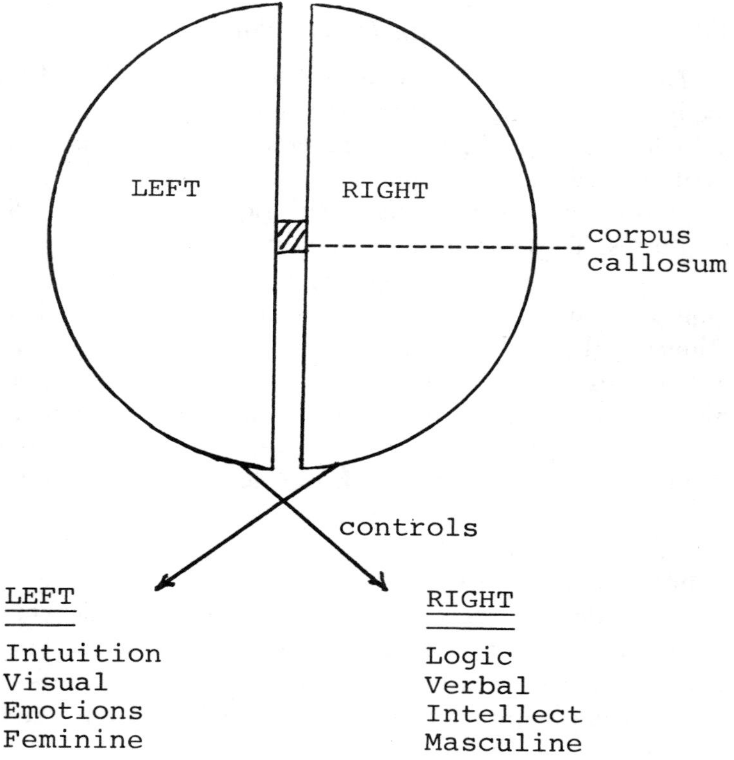

or infoldings on the surface, called convolutions.

The left side of the brain moves or controls the right side of the body. It is the left brain which contributes to an individual's ability to rationalize, to use logic. It is precise and verbal. Remembering names, using math and scientific principles are functions of the left brain. Our Western world has concentrated on left brain development for several hundred years, with the resultant emphasis on technology and left brain attributes. These are usually considered masculine skills.

The right side of the brain operates the left side of the body. The right brain contributes to emotions, relates well to color, music and poetry—the arts. Remembering faces, writing a story and painting are right brain skills. The Eastern world has concerned itself with right brain function for centuries. These are usually called feminine talents.

Chinese[1] and Eastern philosophical and medical disciplines emphasized the differences between left and right. They saw the left brain functions as "yin"—male, dominant, relating to the sun, the giver of energy. The right brain skills were "yang"—female, passive and of the earth, receivers of energy. Their societies were notably male dominated, but also encouraged the development of "feminine" attributes, poetry, art, literature, music. As such, their world tended to be better "balanced" between intellect and intuition than is ours.

A hundred years ago, when the medical practice of bleeding was in vogue, the surgeon was expected to know the differences between left- and right-body ailments. It would have been a grave error to bleed a patient's right arm for a left-body illness!

Fascinating and unexpected results came out of brain surgeries for the control of various types of seizures. When the connection between the two hemispheres, the corpus callosum, was severed, the subjects of this operation developed very separate right/left brain functions. Using the right eye (left brain), one such individual could read the word "table," but not point a table out, nor imagine what one looked like. And when looking out of his left eye (using the right brain), he could draw a picture of a table, and point at one, but was not capable of saying the word. With both eyes open, though, he could make the connections.

Work like this indicated that right and left brain functions were literally separate, and that a person who was a great musician probably used primarily his right brain. Such an artist might find it excruciatingly difficult to think scientifically or logically, simply because he was not encouraged to use his left brain. Likewise, to a mathematician, Van Gogh's use of color may be relatively meaningless!

Even so, this information gives us only one indicator of personal response. Further knowledge begins to complete the picture.

Conscious Mind, Unconscious Mind

So-called "consciousness" and awareness does not reside in the brain. No surgeon can open a skull and pull out consciousness. Neither can he, or she, remove an unconscious or subconscious mind. Where the function of left and right brain belong to medicine, the action of the conscious and unconscious mind are within the province of psychology. Both are important to our study.

The conscious mind, as generally defined, includes the ego, rational thought patterns, self-image (critical faculty) and is goal directed or goal perceiving. That self-image or critical faculty is the individual's accepted ideas about himself—and may not correspond to reality as others see it. A woman might hold a self-image of herself as excessively overweight, where others may believe she is of normal or average weight.

As defined, the unconscious mind, also interchangeably called the subconscious, includes control of the autonomous physical system, symbolic thought patterns, and houses the memory and the goal achieving system. Being symbolism oriented, the unconscious deals well with myths and metaphors, is the seat of the imagination, relates well nonverbally and makes puns.

CONSCIOUS	UN (SUB) CONSCIOUS
1. Ego	1. Autonomous physical system
2. Rational	2. Symbols - imagination
3. Self-image (critical faculty)	3. Memory (T & F)
4. Goal perceiving	4. Goal achieving

Memory is a special area here. It consists of everything the individual has experienced—thoughts, dreams, physical events, feelings, childhood—down to the most minute detail. Thanksgiving at the age of three may consciously be remembered as a fuzzy blur of turkey and cranberry sauce. But stored in that memory, and accessible through hypnosis, are details such as: who was present, their names and how they were dressed, where everyone sat at the table, all the foods that were served and how they tasted (salty, burned, etc.), the time of day dinner was served, how many cars passed the house; topics of conversation, and whatever else occurred! Some say that fetal life and "past" life events are also accessible, but we'll discuss that later.

All past memories can be roughly divided into "true" (T) and "false" (F) thoughts, those references to self which the individual accepts as reality and those he rejects.

Information reaches the T or F portion of the memory by "passing through" the critical faculty. If the data is judged to be correct, it is recorded as true. If experienced as incorrect, it is remembered as false. For example, if I

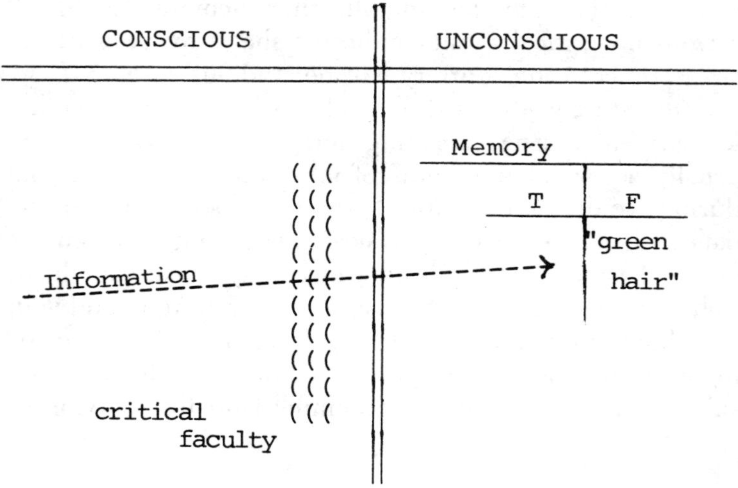

say to you, "Your hair is green," those words will pass through your critical faculty where an instantaneous decision is made as to their validity. Undoubtedly judged untrue, the statement is accurately recorded and remembered as a falsehood. But it is remembered.

In a similar manner if I state "You are male (or female)," a judgment is made and that material memorized as true.

Personal difficulties and confused self-images can arise from details unnecessarily accepted as true. These pieces of information usually come from an authority figure whose ideas are treated uncritically. Mommy says to seven-year-old Robert, "I'm afraid you will never be good at math, dear." Robert may believe that statement as fact, and record it as a piece of correct information. Future mathematics-oriented data is compared to that known "truth"—now a part of the self-image—and correspondingly accepted or rejected.

Whatever is accepted as truth by the critical faculty becomes the basis for judging all other incoming details. If a woman's critical faculty indicates she is overweight, all suggestions to the contrary will be studiously *ignored.*

Interestingly, the critical faculty is lowered or becomes less critical during dreaming and hypnosis. Dreams are usually accorded the status of false after awakening, but during the dream the entire body may react to "imaginary" data as if it was real or physical. Dreaming that you are being chased down a hill by a bear may cause your heart to beat faster, adrenalin to rush into your system, and your breathing rate to increase. The same idea can be suggested hypnotically and—if accepted—can produce the same results. More will be said on dreaming later in this book.

Beliefs and "Reality"

In order to implement changes to an individual's mind, you must understand the particular system you're dealing with. Your client is already confused and tangled amid his difficulties. His life is not working right in some area. He hopes and believes you have some skill that will adjust his problem. A certain awareness and attentiveness to what your client says is the difficulty is important; but then you must look beyond that—if he knew what was really wrong, he would have fixed it already.

Limiting personal beliefs will be part of the problem. Your client has reached a point where he believes he can go no further. His ability to progress is at an end. His thinking will need:

1. support (or a push) or
2. re-education or
3. re-structuring (long term life reorganization).

An unwritten code wisely states that you work no

"deeper" than the subject's overt problem. If he wants only to stop smoking—but shows other unrelated personal problems—you only work on that push to quit smoking, not his total life structure.

Within the function of the conscious and unconscious minds, housed within the left and right brains, are personal beliefs. A belief can be as simple as "I can't understand modern art," or as complex as "God has given me a mandate to kill evil people."

Belief systems are the buoyant material of the unconscious mind and are reflected in all the individual's actions and thoughts. What one's *persona* believes to be true IS truth for them. A belief is not necessarily "reality"—it is one version of reality.[2]

Beliefs act as lenses through which all experience is viewed, and are similar to the "true" portion of memory. Anything encountered will be first sifted through personal beliefs, then accepted or rejected accordingly. Material that is rejected is utterly ignored. The mind is extremely selective in its choice of data—a new mother can hear her baby's cry over the sound of a raucous party—and can refuse to deal with information contradictory to reality as it is understood.

Interestingly, the same mind can hold conflicting beliefs—"I am a good Christian" and "I am a good soldier"—with all that each implies by allowing one belief to dominate. Hence, in the example given, the subject is a fine, churchgoing individual who deeply respects the value of life, yet is able to do whatever is required of him in combat.

Belief systems are tangible forces at work in each person's mind. A belief might be seen as resting in the unconscious, just as a plant's vital root system is "underground," with resultant effects experienced in the conscious mind, "above ground."

Such an inner belief—for example "Money is bad" (sur-

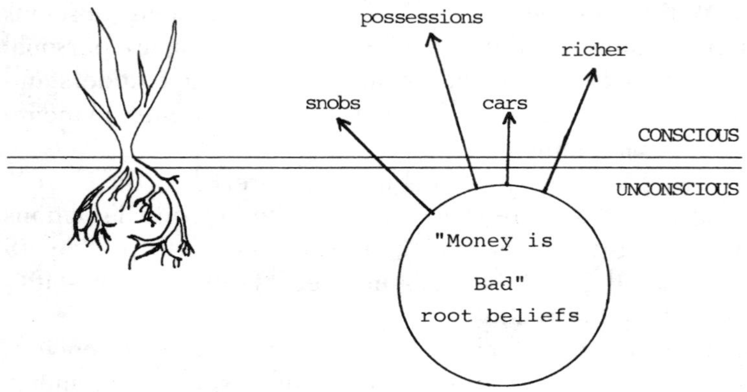

prisingly a popular one)—would not be directly apparent. But the outgrowth of that belief would be. The results might be, "Rich people are snobs," "Big cars pollute the environment," "Material possessions tie you down," "The rich get richer." Consequently, such a person may automatically dislike anyone who possesses whatever he terms wealth—if money is bad, so must be those who have it! A relatively simple belief like this one usually is connected to a specific second series of beliefs. If the individual holds the belief that "I am good," along with "Money is bad," the obvious occurs: he never has enough money. While these beliefs are in force, he will have money only if it becomes "good" or he becomes "bad."

In a similar manner, some members of the medical profession, through years of training and experience, develop beliefs which center on disease. They begin to believe that illness is the primary nature of things, and that good health is an elusive, nearly impossible goal. Such practitioners may feel as though they are fighting a losing battle with sickness—that the bodies of their patients must be bolstered against every flu strain and virus which passes through the area. Again, the individual's belief is going to govern his experience in such a way that information to the contrary is rejected or ignored. This doctor may never see a genuinely healthy person in his life, simply because he never looks for one. Remember, this is a belief about reality, not reality itself.

Successful hypnosis must be carried out within the subject's belief structure. If John believes he is worthless, no amount of hypnosis to the contrary will be effective. However, having John specifically define his worthlessness prior to the induction will help him uproot his entire belief structure. That happens because he begins to experience the belief in conjunction with opposing beliefs. Something has to give. In the following example, notice how the hypnotist indirectly challenges the client's belief in his lack of motivation:

Client: I just can't seem to get myself going!
Hypnotist: How do you mean?
C: You know . . . I've got no motivation. I've gotta be pushed.
H. Got to?
C: Well, yes.
H: How do you have to be pushed to get started?
C: Well, somebody has to tell me to do something—give me instructions.
H: You mean you never do anything unless somebody tells you to do it?

C: (after a pause) I guess I do some things without being pushed. Coming here, for instance.

This particular client went on to describe his belief that he was not progressing quickly enough on the job. Once that information—his real reason for wanting assistance—was known, it was clear what his hypnosis needs were. Suggestions were given that he could work a little more productively each day, which he accepted and then acted on. Specificity counts!

Unconscious Communications

In the pre-hypnosis conversation with your clients you may notice any number of unique personal mannerisms. Many of these apparently meaningless movements, weight shifts and body positions can give you a clearer picture of the client than his words do. This is not body language, as Julius Fast[3] describes it, but it is a close relative. The hypnotist must be aware of what is being said and also what the client's body is doing. Crossed arms, tension, nervous movements, skin color changes, breathing rate, blinking of the eye, lower lips changes—all have their own special connotations.

These bits of communication are "unconscious," that is, outside the person's usual realm of awareness. The subject does not notice what he is doing; his mannerisms are carried out largely by unconscious mechanisms. It might be compared to the inner and outer belief systems, each having their own say simultaneously.

As illustration, suppose the client says, "I really love my wife," all the while shaking his head "no." Consciously, he is aware of the traditional ideas about marriage, and believes he should love his wife. Unconsciously, he doesn't really love her at all. Similarly, an "I'll never do anything like that," accompanied by a nod indicates that the speaker certainly will!

If your client seems relaxed, yet keeps one fist tightly clenched, you can suspect that his relaxation for some reason does not extend there. If this is pointed out, some people will be able to relate their "signal" with an inner thought or feeling previously only expressed that way, i.e., "I could let my boss have it." Drawing attention to the mannerism, on the other hand, may make the client defensive and hostile. Simple observation will produce good results until you have enough rapport with your client to sympathetically bring his attention to the non-verbal communication.

In each preceding situation, the client is sending two contradictory messages. Ordinarily, you would only receive the verbal one. People who suffer severe confusion—schizophrenics and so forth—generally send such a stream of opposing messages that even non-professionals know there is something wrong—often without knowing how! Many signals sent unconsciously are received unconsciously, but reacted to nevertheless. If you find yourself feeling nervous or angry toward a client, and not really sure of the source of your feeling, pay extra attention to the unconscious physical communication going on. You'll find the answer there.

The Eyes

Eyes are an especially important indicator of unconscious thoughts. The difference between dull, glassy eyes and clear, sparkling eyes are one obvious sign that eyes provide—an insight into physical health.

Pupillary dilation is another factor to be considered. It is common knowledge that a contracted pupil is part of the body's autonomic system, protecting the inner eye from, say, bright sunlight. It is also a way to block an offending sight out. Hence, pupillary contraction while discussing a particular topic reveals an unconscious aversion to it. Likewise, pupil dilation shows an attraction. The dilated pupil is open, both figuratively and literally, and consequently you react to it better.

Eye movements during conversation also display unconscious thought patterns as illustrated in the diagram below: When your subject looks upward (that is, with the irises

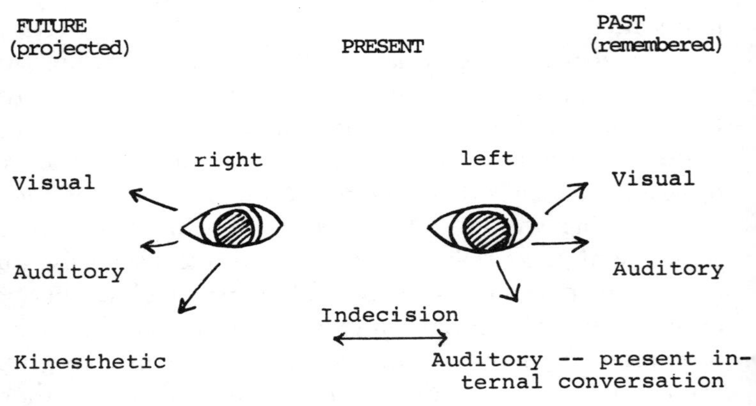

NOTE: Diagram shows subject's responses from <u>your</u> viewpoint.

in approximately the upper third of the eyes) while concentrating, he is using his visual abilities. When he looks downward (with irises in the lower third of the eye) he is experiencing feeling or sound. When the irises are in the middle third of the eye, he is dealing with the present moment. Rapid eye movements back and forth during conversation is an indicator of confusion. During hypnosis, however, rapid eye movements (REM) with the eyes closed indicate that the subject is "viewing" a mental scene. As with reading English, movement of past to future is a left to right progression, so that past feelings or thoughts cause the eye to move to the left of center. Expected feelings or thoughts, or projections of them, will place the iris to the right of center. (This is, of course, the client's right and left.) Center-positioned irises put your client in the present. You can test this by asking some friends to recall a favorite piece of music or do a math problem, and watch where their eyes go.

So, if your client is looking down and to *his* left, you can be certain he is rehearing past sounds. When asked a question such as "How would you feel if X happened?" the subject may glance down left, then down right: this tells you that he first explored his previous verbalizations on the matter, then projected them into feelings. In the same way, if asked to complete a three-digit subtraction problem, the subject will glance upward and either to the left or middle (depending on schooling), then to the right with the solution.

One hypnotist, Steven Heller, Ph.D.,[4] who associates many emotions with the unconscious mind, will sometimes ask his clients to look down right during the pre-hypnosis conversation. This keeps the client in contact with his feelings and helps him be aware of any emotional changes taking place.

A number of studies[5] have been done which correlate left-looking with increased hypnotizability. The point is that right-brain activity seems to be a little more conducive to hypnosis than left (or intellectual) brain activity. Consequently, with a subject who tends to look more to the left of center, a creative imaginative induction probably will work best. For those who tend to glance predominantly rightward, a direct literal induction would be in order. Information on representational systems follows here naturally: "viewing" a scene results in visual ("I see myself . . .") remarks and so forth.

On several occasions I have had the opportunity to hypnotize people who are blind. This creates a certain amount of frustration, both in determining their thought patterns and approaches, and in watching for the eye-associated changes that occur in hypnosis. One of these clients had been blind since age two, and had two artificial eyes. During our conversation before hypnosis, she sat quietly and stared directly forward. I had to alter much of my induction on the spot, to leave out the "see yourself standing" portions, and during the hypnosis her stare didn't vary. However, a young woman who had only been blind for several years continued to show the appropriate eye patterns for each response, proving to me that "outward" sight was not the basis for these eye movements.

Representational Systems

A final approach to clear interaction with your subject is his unique personal vocabulary. As a culture, we are just beginning to really understand that all people do not think the same way; that each statement, word and phrase has a personal coloration which is the product of a lifetime of experience. Not all people are mentally or physically designed to perform one of the most basic functions of our Western world—to read. But there are apparently three very basic systems of language usage, each of which may be tied in to even deeper personal awareness methods. Without understanding the three following languages, you will find it difficult to hold a decent conversation on your client's level: he or she will literally be speaking a different language!

Visual

The most common type is the *visual* person. He has learned to rely on sight and the connotation that seeing has for him. His primary vocabulary will consist of vision-oriented phrases, such as "I see what you mean," where an indirect reference to sight is included. He uses words which imply seeing in some way and usually out of the context the word itself suggests—like "color." "Her remark really *colored* my reaction," might be used. "That seems *clear*," "Things are *looking* good," "*Show* me how," would be further examples. Not all of his conversation will be visual, but a good part of it will be.

To have taught himself to pay particular attention to visual things, this person will have had in his background one of two basic situations:

1. the sight of something frightening or traumatic (usually repressed) or
2. the need to see something clearly, brought on by punishment or instruction, i.e., not watching for cars while crossing a street and nearly getting hit, or a great appreciation for beautiful sights.

Consequently, an emphasis is placed on seeing throughout this person's growing years, for whatever reason, and he has brought that system of relating to the adult world with him.

When speaking to a person who is primarily visual, your language should correspond to sight expressions: "I would like you to *see* yourself relaxing here."

Auditory

Another system of verbal expressions is used by the *auditory* person. This individual has a special skill and way of relating through sounds. He will be particularly in tune with your inflections and pauses. His vocabulary, like that of the visual person, will reflect his inclination: "I *hear* what you're trying to say," "You don't *sound* like you mean that," "I really *tuned* him out," might be phrases he would use. He also has a certain fondness for his own voice, will tend to be talkative, and when nervous or excited may speak especially fast. This person may also have a unique mannerism where he will rest his head on one hand, fingers pointing at his lips or ear!

The auditory person probably had childhood experiences where hearing was important:

1. parental or sibling arguments which required his constant attention to avoid possible danger or
2. special emphasis on sounds, as in a musically oriented or talkative family.

When giving suggestions or speaking to the auditory person, you will find sound-oriented phrases most quickly accepted: "You can really *tune in* to the *sound* of your breathing."

Kinesthetic

The third system of conversing is the *kinesthetic* one. The kinesthetic person is body- and touch-oriented. Words loaded with feeling connotations are his favorites. He may say, "I can *feel* you're right," "I *grasp* that idea," or "I get in *touch* with that." This person is especially aware of textures, and other people's moods. If you are tense or anxious, he will probably know it. He may have a habit of self-touching, such as rubbing his hands together, smoothing his hair, or biting his fingernails—forms of comfort and reassurance. He may also place special emphasis on food and eating, and may tend to be overweight.

The kinesthetic's childhood experiences made touch and feeling important to him, either by:

1. excessiveness, such as physical punishment, or
2. by its lack—the child was not held and touched enough.

You speak to the kinesthetic person through his feelings and body movements: "You can *feel* that tension *draining* right out."

Bandler and Grinder[6] are the source of the following story:

A man phoned one day complaining, "Doctor, I just can't seem to get a grasp on my life. My strength is draining away and I feel like I will never bounce back."

He was answered: "I feel that together the two of us can wrestle this problem to the ground. We can hand you back your energy and cut that problem down to size."

To which the man replied, "Thank you, doctor—you're the first person who really understood me!"

The point I'm getting at here is that the hypnotist spoke in the vocabulary (kinesthetic) the client used. And it was effective.

No individual is exclusively visual, auditory or kinesthetic, however. There is a continuous overlap of language usage, and the individual's subjective moods will color every statement.

During the hypnotic induction, once you have determined your subject's type, you can enhance the effectiveness by gradually changing your phrasing from his primary type to his secondary type, the system he uses to complement the first. This will tend to emphasize his more unconscious elements, and assist the hypnotic process.

To summarize, each client comes to you with a series of difficulties which he believes he cannot solve. Before you even begin the first intimations of a formal hypnotic procedure, you must really understand what your client is saying, and what he wants.

This can be done by paying strict attention to his system of relating to the world. Does he handle logic well? Can he think in visual abstracts? How can you phrase your thoughts and suggestions so that they have the most beneficial effect?

By noting your client's eye movements, you can ascertain whether he tends to intellectualize, or deals with the world through his emotions. If he is rational above all else, you may need to explain what you're doing before he'll play along. If he is emotional by nature, trust your intuitions and suggest he do the same.

As you discuss his situation, notice where he limits himself with a series of restrictive beliefs. Specificity here becomes your key to unlocking these barriers, and you help provide the guidance he believes he requires.

You note where his primary verbalization places his attention. Then you speak to him on that level.

Now you are approaching your client in such a way that he will see/hear/feel safety in your actions. His faith in you will increase; you're relating to him more clearly than anyone has before, simply because you are letting him show you how to do it!

There are only a few more considerations before you begin the actual hypnosis.

NOTES TO CHAPTER TWO

1 This concept is illustrated by the *I Ching: Book of Change* by John Blofeld (E. P. Dutton & Co., 1965).

2 Jane Roberts states these ideas eloquently in *The Nature of Personal Reality: A Seth Book* (Prentice-Hall, 1974).

3 Worthwhile reading, nevertheless! *Body Language* by Julius Fast (M. Evans & Co., Inc., 1970).

4 Steven Heller, Ph.D., of Sherman Oaks, California, is rapidly being hailed the "new Milton Erickson." He has developed extensive and very useful theories on these topics. I have heard that he is working on a book, but currently has no plans for publication.

5 *Trance and Treatment* by Spiegel and Spiegel (Basic Books, 1978) devotes a great deal of space to listing studies done in all areas of hypnosis.

6 Bandler and Grinder have written a number of very useful texts, among which is the forthright *Frogs into Princes, Neurolinguistic Programming* (Real People Press, 1979).

CHAPTER THREE

The Hypnotizer's Philosophy

I settled comfortably into the reclining chair in my eminent colleague's office. It was my third session with Dr. S., and I fully believed that our work together was doing good things for me. Like most people who go to a hypnotist, I was feeling powerless to solve several personal problems; I hoped he could help me find direction.

My colleague is a very intelligent man. He had to fight his way—all the way—to a very high position of respectability. I now suspect that somewhere in me he saw the forces he had been fighting against—the questioners and doubters. Or perhaps I am being too generous in assessing what transpired in those few moments, but it was to become the deciding factor in our work together.

Dr. S. pulled several sugar cubes from a packet in his desk. I knew instantly what he had planned: I'd watched him perform the same "test" several weeks before. He would want me to take a cube in my mouth and let it dissolve, while he tested the strength in my arms. This would supposedly show him my physical reaction to sugar—and whether I was hypoglycemic or not. What he didn't know was that I had been doing this "sugar trick" with my classes for several years, and that, like Luys and Charcot before us, we had found that sometimes even the proximity of sugar could produce weakness in susceptible people. "Susceptible" translates here into "suggestible."

"Take this," he said, "and stand up."

"I know what you're doing, but I won't take it," I answered. I had spent the prior month avoiding sugar in all forms to determine my own reactions to it . . . and using a little self-hypnosis to encourage myself.

"What?" he said, as if he hadn't heard me.

"I'm conditioned against it," I explained.

"What do you mean?" he asked, becoming agitated.

"I'm conditioned against it—I haven't had a speck of sugar in over a month . . ."

"You're not going to do this!" he said tersely, cutting me off.

I tried to make him understand, "I haven't had . . ."

"All right!" he snapped. "I'm sick of people refusing to help themselves! Don't do it!"

By now I was embarrassed. How could I possibly ignore his expressed desire to help? The session continued—for me, uneasily—and I was relieved when it was time to leave.

Will and Choice

In those few moments, Dr. S. unwittingly trespassed into my personal private territory, my free will. I thoroughly believed I was doing the right thing for myself by leaving sugar out of my diet—and he expected me to do the opposite of what I felt was best. Then, adding insult on top of it, he essentially said that doing what I thought was best was, in fact, a rude refusal to help myself! I still cannot understand at what point he concluded that what he wanted for me was better than what I wanted for myself. And all along I'd thought we both were working for my betterment!

Many of us, in our zealous desire to "help," do the same thing—step on the rights and privileges of others because we believe what we are doing is right. Each client, each person, still has the ultimate choice, the final word based on free will in deciding what is to be accepted and what is not.

That idea is still lacking in many professional circles. One doctor smugly announced on a health-oriented TV program that "people don't have the capacity to judge their state of health," implying that only he and other medical men had that ability! That man may be surprised to learn that I actually know when I have a head cold, or when I feel tired. I really don't need his assistance to confirm my suspicions. Nor did I need to be told when I was pregnant with my first child: something in me let me know within the first two weeks. Many women experience the same thing, often quite some time before medical procedures can determine the fact.

Yet, will and choice are the prerogative of the individual. When you attempt to violate that right, as Dr. S. did, you create a state of distrust between your client and yourself. If I was acting in my best interest, and Dr. S. wanted me to violate that, was he not actually asking me to act against myself? And if I had agreed to complete the test, I—like anyone—would have felt resentment and anger that my desires and needs had been ignored.

The emphasis on belief systems in the last chapter is directly applicable here. Each person holds a unique world view, and it is not the therapist's job—whether hypnotist, doctor or psychologist—to forcibly dissuade them. Dr. S. and I were sufficiently adult to have calmly discussed what we both believed was best. Had we done that, I'm certain we could have reached a point of concurrence. In a similar manner, if you ask (notice "ask" rather than "want") your client to do something and he refuses, you have probably stepped on his beliefs. If he knows why he doesn't want to do that thing, you can both analyze it reasonably. We're dealing here with individuals who are in normal possession of their faculties. It is not within the purview of this volume to discuss the treatment of numerous unusual mental disorders. However, the highly disturbed people I've worked with in the past have indicated that the act of making their own choices—even if that decision led to complications—was something they had been denied in the past. The act of making those choices seemed to be a necessary step in their growth.

The same applies to the hypnotized subject. His sense of free will and choice may even be clearer to him. *He knows* what he wants to do, and not do. You literally cannot force someone to go against their will, hypnosis or not. The hypnotist is strictly a guide who can indicate the benefits of certain actions—not a slave driver.

Certainly, if your client is already predisposed to bank robbery, and you suggest hypnotically that he rob a bank, you are not asking for a violation of belief systems. You may suggest to a murderer that he kill, or that a smoker go ahead and smoke. He has already demonstrated that these things are normal for him. When hypnotized, your client will not do anything he would not ordinarily do.

The hypnotized person does not lose touch with his surroundings. He does not become "unconscious" or forget his name or location (though some may choose not to recall the contents of a session immediately afterwards). He may actually become hyperaware! Being in hypnosis feels very similar to being wide awake, except that attention is focused more sharply. Hypnosis is very much a consent state. A subject must agree at some level to cooperate with you. But that cooperation extends only as far as he chooses.

At one time I was asked to act as a test subject for a group of doctors studying hypnosis. Their experiments were to be conducted by the respected John Gilkerson, D.C., a hypnotist and chiropractor in Glendale, California. Having seen Dr. Gilkerson in action before, I had the utmost faith in his technique—it wasn't even necessary to discuss the test procedures.

While hypnotized, I sat at a school desk on a platform. There were about twenty interested spectators. I knew at all times exactly what Dr. Gilkerson was doing, yet, I freely chose to respond to his requests, in whatever way possible.

At one point, Dr. Gilkerson instructed me to numb my sinuses. To my knowledge, I had never had a set of numb sinuses before, but I tried to imagine them shut down for repairs. I saw him break an ammonia inhalant capsule and place it in a plastic flower. I realized that I would be sniffing it shortly. When he brought it up to my nose, I was able to inhale deeply—and I responded as if my sinuses were numb!

Later on in the demonstration, he suggested that the back of my right hand would remain relaxed, and that nothing done to it would bother me in the least. At that point I recall being a little nervous about what he planned to do to my hand. I also remember thinking that I'd just better get it right! He asked me to close my eyes. I clearly heard him open a sterile pack for a syringe needle. I felt the pressure of the needle against the skin of my right hand, then felt it slip effortlessly under the skin surface and out again about an inch away. I heard members of the class gasp and walk over for a closer look. It didn't hurt in the least, though I did feel a kind of pressure. Mostly, I was amazed that it worked so well!

Dr. Gilkerson then asked me to choose "one side or the other"—the entry or exit holes—for my hand to bleed from. With a kind of mental shrug, I picked the innermost puncture, not knowing exactly how I would fulfill that suggestion. When he removed the needle, the puncture I'd chosen did bleed: one long stream which I felt drip down my hand. It stopped when he said it was sufficient!

Quite simply, it was the act of volition which allowed each step of the process to work. Had I, at any time, become frightened or chosen not to continue, the demonstration would have had to stop.

This can be illustrated by another personal experience—one not so positive, but equally instructive. An older man, who had some limited hypnotic experience, and I were experimenting on each other with various induction techniques. We were quite secluded from possible interruption. I hypnotized him and then we discussed his subjective viewpoint, what seemed to work and what didn't. Next, he hypnotized me. I was enjoying the peaceful imagery of drifting down a stream in a canoe, relaxed and at ease. Suddenly, to my disbelief, he attempted to force himself on me. Just as suddenly, I was out of hypnosis and had my fist planted against his chest. My choice and free will were being violated—and I would not stand for it!

Needless to say, having had an experience like that, I have a special interest in alleged "hypnotic rape" cases. Some people use hypnosis as a "scapegoat" for many questionable traits and actions, and often explain themselves by simply saying "I had to. I was hypnotized." Included in this category is the woman who under hypnosis becomes seductive. She may actually expose herself to the male hypnotist—and insist afterwards that hypnosis made her do it! In truth, if an otherwise normal woman submits to a hypnotist's amorous advances while in hypnosis, it is because she has chosen to do just that. It's a safe choice, too . . . who would question her statement that she was hypnotized and couldn't escape?

It is a sorry fact that more cases are coming to light where therapists in every field are taking advantage of the trust of their clients. William Kroeger, M.D., mentioned previously, has said that hypnosis *per se* is not dangerous, but it is the persuasive complexities of deep human relationships which can lead to problems. In other words, trust and belief can be put into anyone—the milkman or school teacher—with disastrous results, too.

Again, because hypnotism is so misunderstood, it can become an excuse for extreme behavior. My favorite example of this was a man who came walking into my office one spring morning. He was an intelligent, reasonably pleasant young man. Very calmly, as he leaned back in the reclining chair, he described how he had been hypnotized by "them" to forget how to spell. Furthermore, they had hypnotized him to become a homosexual, and to attack anyone else who attempted to hypnotize him. And he had been hypnotized in Latin. He implored me to hypnotize him out of all these difficulties. I promptly sent him to an excellent psychologist who diagnosed him as a paranoid schizophrenic. I've heard he is doing much better now. I also learned that he had never been hypnotized in his life!

It should also be clearly established at this point that the subject's unconscious mind can choose and make important decisions without his conscious awareness. However, this does not negate the aspects of free will and choice. It places choice on a more internal level. Conscious cooperation is still utilized. You may, for example, have the person "go inside" and make an agreement with the "habit part" or whatever, for the good of the whole. More on this in Chapter Six.

Self-Responsibility

Our culture is entering an age of increased self-responsibility. In the 1950's and 60's, it was fashionable, even acceptable, to rely on the miraculous advances of medicine. Barbiturates and amphetamines became a way of life for some, complemented by the assurance that everything would work out right—without any awareness of the underlying problems involved. By 1970, changes were already apparent. An entire "home-birth" movement was established; many young people hesitated to follow the tradition of dropping their bodies off for shots or to be prescribed pills to be picked up an hour later; "urban flight" was underway.

A portion of these changes came from the developing concept that a person might sometimes create an illness for its own advantage. Psychosomatics, the study of mental and emotional effects on physical health, gained an increasing number of professional converts. Perhaps it wasn't only viruses and germs which caused disease; perhaps the individual *needed* to be sick—as an excuse, as a comfort, as a method of controlling others, as a way of getting attention, to experience illness or even as a protection from the outside world.

In 1974, Drs. Meyer Friedman and Ray Rosenman's book, *Type A Behavior and Your Heart*[1], created an instant sensation. Their extensive work had shown that certain coronary artery disease was brought about by emotional factors—notably hostility, "time urgency" and aggression.

Heart problems could be triggered by the way you treat yourself! Conversely, by being responsible for one's own health, certain illnesses could be avoided.

Self-responsibility, then, is just as the name implies: an awareness for and caring about oneself. Various individuals have various ways of being self-responsible. This is intimately connected with their beliefs in their personal "power" over life situations. Ordinarily, if a pin were put through the back of my hand, my beliefs indicate that it would hurt—and I probably wouldn't sit calmly waiting for someone to do it to me. My sense of self-responsibility would make it imperative for me to get away from that potential "danger." Yet, while allowing my beliefs to "expand" under hypnosis—that is, when believing completely in Dr. Gilkerson's statement that it wouldn't hurt—I quite literally made *him* responsible for my reactions. Like a mother who kisses her child's scrape to make it better, he "promised" me it would be okay. By choosing to accept that idea, I withdrew my own responsibility for my own behavior. My trust was well placed.

To some degree, each of us does this daily. We innocently trust our mail to the post office, with the faith that they will deliver it as they have promised. We trust the dentist's judgment that certain things must be done to our teeth. We believe the doctor's diagnosis. We trust our teachers to provide the "truth." Likewise, a client needs faith in the hypnotist.

A hypnotist can fail more readily if he says the wrong thing, in the wrong way, than a dentist or a doctor can. He is working more intimately with his client's beliefs. He needs that belief in him, and needs the client to temporarily volunteer his sense of responsibility to him.

It must be the goal of each hypnotist to reinstall the client's sense of personal power as part of the hypnotic process. If nothing else, I'll end each hypnosis with "you can feel better about yourself every day" to encourage that. But the typical people who come to see me do so because they hold a belief in the power of hypnosis, and a concurrent belief in their own powerlessness in dealing with their problem. It is difficult or nearly impossible to explain that I personally have no innate power, no magic formula which will rid them of their afflictions. Common sense must show that all I really do is sit in a chair and talk. I do make use of their idea of my imagined omnipotence to activate their own self-help mechanisms. If my clients need to believe that I "make" them lose weight or stop smoking—if they surrender that much self-responsibility to me, then so be it. But I make a point of answering all the "you made me see the light" remarks with "It only worked because you let it."

In a way, we're still talking about hypnosis as an excuse for specific behavior. By hypnotizing a client, you provide him with an excuse to use his previously denied personal strengths.

You as a hypnotist must never, therefore, fall into the trap of believing that you have some skill or power which saves or cures. You literally do nothing but suggest. There is nothing more inappropriate than seeing an egocentric hypnotist bragging about all the wonderful things he's made people do. He just doesn't know what he's talking about.

A thought about choice: not everyone really wants to have problems solved, illnesses cured, or obstacles overcome. There are therapy "burnouts," people who have been the round of est, Silva, Scientology, Hypnosis, Esalen, Arica etc. A man wants hypnosis to help him stop smoking, but prefaces the session by saying, "I'm only here because my wife forced me to come. I really don't think it will work." And it won't. These people are the real trial of any therapist—and particularly the hypnotist.

An example of this comes to mind. An 83-year-old woman was referred to me by her daughter. The woman had just been removed from a convalescent home by the daughter's family. The daughter believed her mother was simply in too good health—mentally and physically—to quietly vegetate away her final years. I worked with the mother, and found that she was in excellent health, had a strong desire to resume normal living, and accepted the belief that I could help. The daughter and I both encouraged, cajoled and helped the mother to regain her ability to walk, cook and carry on her daily duties. It was also one of the longest cases I've ever worked, lasting over a year of twice weekly sessions.

The mother progressed beautifully during that time. She became increasingly more self-responsible, and was even able to attend a grandson's wedding. Abruptly, problems in the daughter's personal life called her away. While the mother held on to her sense of power for a time, she became more and more complaining. She missed the extra attention her daughter gave. Small occurrences, such as dropping a cup, took on major proportions, and became signs that she was "going backward." One morning, she gave up her self-responsibility with a dramatic gesture. She slipped from bed, without injury, onto the floor and utterly refused to stand up alone again. Where she had been an "I can do anything" person before, she became an "I can't." Her health remained excellent and her mind active—but she concentrated solely on *not* doing anything. She chose not to help herself, much to the consternation of everyone involved. At this writing, she is back in another rest home, still in outstanding physical condition, and still choosing inactivity. It is difficult for me to face the fact that this woman has decided to give up the life she could have had.

Yet, it is her choice and I have no right to tell her otherwise. I could help as long as she let me, but that time is over.

The client's decisions deserve the same respect as your own personal choices do. If they choose failure, and choose not to accept assistance, you must grant them the dignity of their refusal. It is, after all, their life.

THE RULES OF THE GAME

Keeping in mind the considerations of free will and self-responsibility, several basic principles of mental functioning arise. These rules can provide a guideline to what the client will accept from you and what he will not, as well as possibly why:

1. *The mind is self-protective*. This rule is far more pervasive than we can imagine. Each mind will attempt to defend itself from whatever is perceived as threatening. This defense may consist of repression of traumatic material, unconsciousness, catatonia, complete amnesia, bizarre altered states of consciousness, religious visions, madness, and so forth. Cases of multiple personality, such as the much-publicized *Sybil*[2], show how strong the self-protective rule is. When the young Sybil's mother perpetrated physical and mental cruelties on the child, Sybil developed a new self to handle each hurt—beginning before she was three years old. Protecting the "real Sybil" was accomplished by having Sybil "1" (Peggy) feel sadness or pain, for example. This can be loosely compared to a large corporation creating independent divisions to handle its various products (see next page).

Each "division" operates within specific limits, and sends its reports to the central "control" on a regular basis. Each section, however, has its own "memory bank," which may or may not overlap others, but all information is simultaneously stored at "headquarters."

Unexpressed talents may act as a source of mental or physical tension. Confined talents, like confined anger, build an inescapable emotional/psychological pressure that can lead to neurosis, psychosis and the like. So the artist must paint, just as the tormented juvenile must vandalize. Both act in a self-preserving manner.

Jane Roberts, in her excellent *Adventures in Consciousness: An Introduction to Aspect Psychology*[3], discusses her

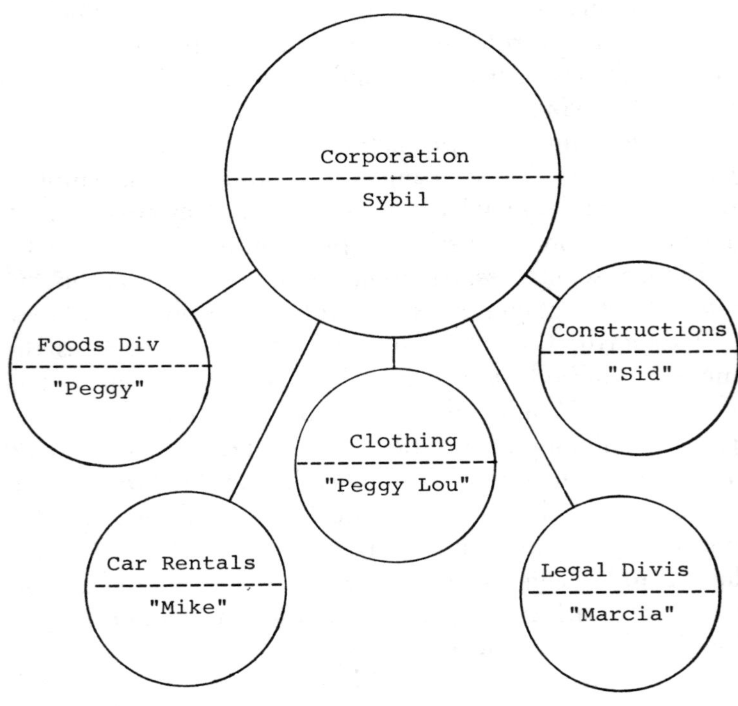

contacts with individuals who experience the pressure of unexpressed talents. Some claim personal encounters with UFOs, others impersonate various historical religious figures. She states:

> The exaggerations in such communications are probably in direct proportion to the person's previous inner desperation, and represent the tormenting need to free inner energies. These, then, take on the cloak of any ideas or persons in whom the individual has confidence, and thereby allow a belief and acceptance of concepts that the recipient would be afraid to entertain on his or her own authority.[4]

. . . in the interest of preserving the self. If the subject's life situation is experienced as potentially deadly—whether or not it is to the observer—insanity may be preferable to death. From this a generalization may be drawn: individual difficulties are the results of attempting to avert what seemed a worse alternative. Thus the client killed himself rather than go mad, or became an alcoholic because it was better than being sober!

2. *The mind is goal directed*. That is, without a specific goal, there is no direction. With this rule, action itself can become a goal: getting up in the morning is as much a goal as getting the big contract for the company. A person may hold a long-term or short-term goal, or goals may overlap. It can be either beneficial or destructive—still seen within the framework of self-protection, of course. Continuing failure in relationships may be one man's goal—because it protects him from the rigors of intimacy.

3. *Each expression of the mind is significant*. Body language and graphology both hold this rule to be fundamental. "Expression" here may be verbal, artistic, physical, conscious or without the client's awareness. Each expression reflects an attitude, a belief, agreement or disagree-

ment, level of contact with emotion, rapport with the hypnotist and so on. When you begin to pay attention to people's innumerable modes of expression, you will have touched on the psyche's rich communication system—and you may be surprised at how vast it really is. This is covered fully in Chapters Four and Six.

4. *The mind seeks to reply to all questions posed.* But that reply may come as any one of the multitudinous physical, mental, emotional or symbolic expressions. The reply usually arrives rapidly, but takes time and effort to unravel and understand.

5. *The mind understands itself.* That is, the individual's inner mind knows what choices were made, what alternative accepted or rejected, to reach the point at which it currently exists. This is usually not known at a conscious level. John Woodbury, Ph.D., describes such a situation in his case study on incest,[5] where his hypnotized patient analyzes her dreams, actions and feelings in detail. Woodbury is careful to allow his subject all the internal protection she requires: he helps her establish a secondary personality to undergo traumas "for" her, and suggests amnesia for details she had trouble coping with. Nothing, however, is truly forgotten—everything is simply made inaccessible until the material can be tolerated.

These five basic rules boil down to one single thought: respect for your client's personality. Milton Erickson insists that no force be used in hypnosis, no demands or ultimatums made. This allows the subject free will for his self-benefit. By dealing directly with your client's belief systems, you can open the doorway to his ultimate free will.

Dangers of Hypnosis

There are no dangers inherent in the act of hypnotizing—no more than there are dangers in a sales presentation, a sermon or a political speech.

When it is clearly understood that the hypnotized subject is *not* a victim of the hypnotist's power, the question of "danger" becomes meaningless. Can an individual unknowingly harm himself?

There *will* be a danger to your clients only if they ascribe to you the infallible power of the gods, and negate their own strengths. The danger here is that they can lose proper perspective of their abilities.

There will be a danger to you, in hypnotizing, if you are frightened by your client's displays of emotion, have an affair with a client (hypnotized or not), or forget the limits of your responsibilities.

The cases where a hypnotist supposedly has forced a subject to kill or commit immoral acts seldom deal with the subject's motives. The Candy Jones case[6] is a prime example of a subject's compliance and willingness to follow instructions to the disagreeable letter—in this situation, her compliance came from her feelings of patriotism. Sadly enough, many people have done worse things than Candy Jones did in the name of patriotism—and without the aid of a hypnotist.

To repeat, hypnotism itself is not dangerous. There is danger only in placing unfailing trust in unscrupulous people, whomever they may be.

Now, with the next chapter, you can begin hypnotizing.

Notes to Chapter Three

1 *Type A Behavior and Your Heart* by Friedman and Rosenman (Knopf, 1974).
2 *Sybil* by Flora Schreiber (Warner Books, 1974).
3 *Adventures in Consciousness, an Aspect Psychology Book* by Jane Roberts (Prentice-Hall, 1975)
4 Ibid., page 191
5 *The Silent Sin* by John Woodbury, Ph.D., and Elroy Schwartz (New American Library, 1971)
6 *The Control of Candy Jones* by David Bain (Playboy Press, 1976). I especially like this because it aptly demonstrates the extent to which one mind can be "bent"—almost like a created, controlled insanity.

CHAPTER FOUR

Inducing Hypnosis: The Journey Inward

The act of hypnotizing is probably the very simplest part of the entire hypnosis phenomenon. Each person passes through a hypnotic state at least twice a day—once on awakening (the hypnopompic) and once on returning to sleep (the hypnagogic)—and usually more often than that. Television is a wonderful hypnotic medium, as are music, sound effects, day-dreaming, concentration, and a host of other ordinary activities. Anytime a person becomes involved with a movie or book and feels an emotional reaction, he has placed himself into hypnosis.

It is such an entirely natural state that many people undergoing formal hypnosis for the first time insist that they did not "feel" hypnotized, without being able to define just how hypnosis feels.

Good induction technique consists, then, primarily of having a certain confidence in what you are saying.

General Considerations

When inducing hypnosis in a first time client, it should be made very clear to the subject what to expect—and what not to expect. Failure to do this can be the root of all manner of difficulties in following sessions. You should make a point of defining hypnosis (i.e., "pleasant state of relaxation") and demystifying it as much as possible. People still expect to blank out or lose control of themselves when hypnotized, so by eliminating those ideas from the start, you avoid having to pacify someone who thinks they "didn't do it right" because they could still hear your voice.

Hypnosis is not a miracle cure, although there have been some spectacular results in the past. It is common to take three sessions before the client feels comfortable enough with you to really open up—and eight sessions before appreciable work is done. I try to be sure that the client understands that each session builds on the previous one, and that a "miracle"—though they do happen—is unlikely. This prepares the client for ready acceptance of the work that must be done.

Outside distractions should be kept at a minimum. Take phones off hooks or otherwise disconnect them. Post a "SHHH . . . Hypnosis in Progress" sign conspicuously. Tell family and friends to keep radios and televisions low. Your own concentration will need to be at its finest level, especially in the first sessions of hypnosis you give. For the client's benefit, the less outside noise, the better—but it is certainly possible to continue practicing hypnosis in a noisy area, if you condition the client beforehand. My office is currently located on a busy street corner, where traffic sounds and barking dogs create a steady, dull background noise. I tell the client that he may notice the amount of things happening during the first session, but in each succeeding session, the noise will become less and less important. It has worked extremely well.

The induction itself should be expressed in a tone of utmost confidence—firmly but soothingly. The impression you give here will be important, because your subject is grasping each word with a clarity and understanding scarcely possible when not in hypnosis. If you sound weak or unsure, he will pick it up and react accordingly. If you sound harsh or demanding, your client may be put off and refuse to cooperate. The rate or speed of the induction should be according to the client's individual needs, gradually slowing down to match his breathing rate. I've found that stating a brief sentence or part of a sentence with each of the subject's exhalations times the induction perfectly. Exhaling is already a relaxing process, and coupled with a relaxing thought produces good results.

The Process

In the entire process of a hypnosis session, the induction is only one component of an overall picture, consisting of:

1. pre-conditioning
2. induction
3. suggestions
4. suggestions for re-hypnosis
5. awakening

Each step in this formula is as vital to the success of the session as any other.

Pre-conditioning: This consists of the client's entire exposure to hypnosis and to you prior to the actual induction. This will include TV/movie/reading where hypnosis has played a part; all gossip or information he has heard about you; your office setting and any conversation the two of you had beforehand. This is why it can be so difficult to work on family members, particularly parents. You remain "little

Billy or Sally" to them, despite your learning and experience. I make my office as casual and homey as possible, provide coffee or tea and relaxing background music; the client responds by relaxing automatically when he sees I'm not the fearful apparition he expected.

Induction: Conversation has indicated to me that the client is prepared to be hypnotized. He has relaxed, is open to beneficial thoughts, appears to be ready to work. I begin by saying, "Since it's not important to keep your eyes open, you may let them close . . ." and the induction is underway. The induction itself may consist of whatever formula or technique you feel most comfortable with.

Suggestions: Your entire induction has been a series of suggestions to be acted upon immediately. The suggestions you give during this phase of the session will be of longer duration, and some should be expected to continue posthypnotically. Giving suggestions for maximum effect is an art in itself, and is covered in detail in Chapter Six.

Suggestions for re-hypnosis: If you intend to work with a client on a regular basis, it is wise to suggest that with each succeeding session he will be more amenable to hypnosis. "Each time you enter a state of hypnosis, you go into it more deeply, more easily than the previous time," is a statement of fact as well as a suggestion. You may also wish to use a cue of some kind here. "In the future, when I say 'Relax, relax, relax,' you can instantly return to this deep and comfortable state" might be one example of this. It saves the time spent and gets you immediately to the work at hand.

Awakening: This process is as simple as "1–2–3, wide awake!" Anything you suggest will awaken the subject. Actually, "awaken" is not the best choice of words, because the subject has not been asleep; but conventional terms are acceptable here. I prefer a longer awakening process, allowing the subject to bring himself out of hypnosis at his own rate, something like: "Now slowly and agreeably, bring yourself to full and refreshing awakening, feeling alert, revitalized and comfortably at ease." Most bring themselves out of hypnosis within a minute or two. For those who take much longer than that, or who seem to have any hesitation about awakening, I'll usually count slowly and progressively louder from 1 to 10, stating that when I reach ten, they'll be wide awake, feeling wonderful.

Induction Semantics

As part of the overall principle that hypnosis is a consent state, your client's cooperation is essential to success. A dictator does not get cooperation—he gets rebellion, and so it is with the hypnotist. The language you use will convey what sort of a hypnotist you are—whether dictator or supporter. Contrast the different effects in your own mind of the following:

"I want you to relax now."
"Allow yourself to relax now."

When a person is entering hypnosis, the first sentence has a very harsh, commanding tone, no matter how pleasantly said. The usual unconscious answer to this statement is, "Who cares what you want?" It interferes with the subject's free will—he is not undergoing hypnosis to do what you want, but what he wants. On the other hand, the second sentence gets the same point across and gives the subject the right of choice. He doesn't *have* to relax, and he's not resisting *you* if he doesn't. If he resists, he is only fighting himself. This concept should be adhered to throughout the induction; that is, giving the client the opportunity for action, rather than demanding it.

As a matter of principle, I advise avoiding the use of terms such as "sleep" and "trance" to designate the hypnotic state. Hypnosis bears no resemblance to sleep or mediumistic trances, and the terms help to generate false ideas about what will occur. When a client is told that he is going into a deep sleep, yet remains aware of what has happened while hypnotized, he cannot help but doubt the veracity of the hypnotist's claims. Many hypnotists, however, continue to use "sleep" and "trance" as part of their professional vocabulary, making a point to explain that no actual sleep or trances are involved. I believe a common sense approach would be to leave the undesirable language out completely.

Further objectional terms are those which designate pain, stress or loss of control. This would include, "It won't *hurt* for you to relax," "*falling* asleep," "*sinking* into relaxation," "*tension* eases out," and so forth. "Sinking" seems to be particularly evocative for some suggestible people: it has a connotation of helpless drowning, and few enjoy that idea!

It is a good plan to initially train yourself to use words with only "positive" or beneficial meanings. Avoid all "negative" words such as "can't," "won't," "don't," "not," and especially "try." "Try" implies failure—that the subject can *try* to relax (as in, "try, try again"), but the effort will be pointless. "I will try to study" has an entirely different meaning—and outcome—than "I will study." Later, as your hypnotic technique becomes more individualized, you can begin to add words with negative implications. Effectively used, they can add the proper mental question marks—turning a negative statement into a positive suggestion. More on this in Chapter Six.

Also, avoid telling your subject what he is doing, such as "you are relaxing." He already knows what he is doing, and if he isn't relaxing, you've proven yourself a liar. Say instead, "You can relax." The effect is much better, and again, it allows the subject the option of rejecting it, which makes it easier to accept.

Spice your vocabulary with words suggesting pleasurable experience—"relaxation," "comfort," "resting on a cloud," "beautiful lake," the list is endless. You can make each act involved in the hypnosis desirable in this way, so that the subject isn't simply "being hypnotized," he is "going to experience the ease and tranquility of deep, soothing relaxation."

Suggestibility Testing

Testing for subject susceptibility to suggestion is a feature of the hypnotic process which I believe belongs primarily in the domain of stage performance. In a therapeutic setting, you will best find the hypnotizability of your subject by hypnotizing him—not by applying various tests. Nevertheless, suggestibility testing can show some very interesting features of how people respond to "hints" given indirectly by the hypnotist. It is not infallible in determining who will be a good subject and who will not. Only actual hypnosis can do that.

There are several well-known and much used tests for suggestibility. Each has a unique approach: some relying on physical mechanisms, some on the subject's imagination, some on the purely personal interaction between hypnotist and subject. The following are good for experimenting on others—and yourself:

Falling backwards test: As the name suggests, the point is to have the subject fall backward at the designated moment. You stand behind the subject, lightly touching his back. He is asked to stand with heels together, toes apart, and stare directly upward at a spot just above his head. He is told that this is a test to determine how open he will be to hypnosis, and that in a moment, when you pull your hand away from his back, he will sway and fall backwards. You will be there to catch him.

The position the subject is in will automatically throw his whole body off balance. By turning your light touch on his back into a gentle nudge, you'll throw his weight forward—to which he reacts by leaning backwards. At this point, some people will sway precariously, trying to right their balance, eventually assume that they are responding properly, and fall backwards. Others will simply continue backwards, usually physically rigid—with feet remaining at right angles to the body. That person has already gone into hypnosis!

Rock/balloon test: This test works best for imaginative, left-looking people (see Chapter Two). The object of the test is to produce a reaction by imagining a rock in one hand, a balloon attached to the other.

The subject is asked to sit comfortably, and close his eyes. He is asked to stretch out both arms in front of himself at shoulder level, palm of the left hand up, right hand closed with thumb pointing upward. Using his creative imagination, he is to picture, feel and sense a large, heavy rock placed into his left hand weighing it down, and make it as real as possible. Then, similarly create a gigantic, helium-filled balloon, of whatever color he chooses, tied to his right thumb, tugging that right arm gently upward. When an appreciable difference in the height of both hands is noted, he is asked to open his eyes, and see the powerful effects of his own imagination.

Some people respond to this rapidly, others take several minutes to get going. Sometimes, highly responsive people will have sore muscles from "holding up the rock!" If working this test on a group of people, I like to include one line—"Let's see who has the best imagination"—the sense of competition produces better overall results.

Rigid arm test: The purpose of this test is to produce a limb catalepsy. It also indicates whether your subject will follow instructions or not.

The subject is asked to sit comfortably, extend his right arm and look at the tip of his longest finger. Concentrating on that spot, he is to imagine his arm growing longer and longer, and stronger and stronger, until it reaches the opposite wall, grows into it and supports it. He is to imagine that arm supporting an entire 50,000 ton bridge, or other suitable idea of strength. Then, continuing to imagine that arm extended and strong, he is asked to *try* to bend it. If he has followed your instructions, he won't bend it.

There is a good deal of verbal skill required on your part with this one. Basically, you are asking him to do two mutually exclusive things simultaneously—keep the arm straight and bend it at the same time. Use of the word "try" here implies even further that he won't be able to. But don't leave the subject trying for too long, or the impossibility of it will become obvious. End with something to the effect of, "And now, having proven how powerful your will can be, that arm can relax completely back to normal." This test has nearly thirty variations, but I've found this version easiest to implement.

The giving of any suggestibility test does require a certain amount of finesse, something easiest to acquire after having done hypnosis for a while. It can be embarrassing and a source of problems if a test doesn't work properly, especially on a first session. Therefore, I advise use of these only when you're very sure of yourself, and of your subject's likely reactions.

Signs of Hypnosis

As part of the overall process of developing your skills as a hypnotist, you must develop your powers of observation. Any given person who is in the hypnotic state will show characteristic signs of his condition. Not all people evidence the same signs, but each person will have one or more of the following:

1. warm hands
2. change in breathing to regular, deep breaths
3. eyelid flutter
4. eyeballs rolled upward or REM
5. whites of the eyes turning red
6. increased lacrimation (tearing)
7. unconscious or ideomotor response (jerks, spasms)
8. absence of regular swallow reflex, as in sleep
9. slowed physical responses

Probably the most outstanding sign of hypnosis—and the one which is impossible to fake—is the reddening of the whites of the eyes. The physiological reason for this is not clear, but I would suppose the increase in optic blood supply goes with increased relaxation.

In spite of having noticed one or several of these signs in your client, he may have reservations about believing he was actually hypnotized. Reactions you will hear are "I didn't feel any different," "I could have opened my eyes anytime," and "How do you know I was hypnotized?" The last question is easiest to answer, simply by running through the signs of hypnosis the individual showed. The other two statements, and variations of those themes, are harder to resolve. Both reactions indicate the subject still expects hypnosis to be bizarre in one way or another. For the "I didn't feel different" crowd, rather than go through the explanation of hypnosis again, I will ask, "What does hypnosis feel like?" Of course, having never been hypnotized, they don't know. It often shows the client where his expectations have led him astray. To the "I could open my eyes" group, I respond with, "So why didn't you?" However that question is answered can be taken as an indication of the cooperation essential to hypnosis.

All of these difficulties can be avoided early in the induction by including statements and lines which "prove" to the client that he is responding properly. This includes comments such as, "And that feeling of heaviness, or lightness, or numbness, or tingling in your legs is a sign to you that you are actually entering hypnosis."

Progressive Relaxation Induction Form

The Progressive (or Fractional) Relaxation Induction form is the oldest and most basic induction type, from which nearly all other inductions derive their existence. As such, it is fundamental to all hypnotic techniques and the foundation on which more "sophisticated" programs can be built. It is also the simplest (though most lengthy) induction in use today.

The following formula for the PR induction is a general guideline on which the formal ritual can be based. The version that I use is included, but don't succumb to the temptation to use it word for word. No one else's induction will work as well for you as it does for them. Only the one *you* personally develop will be truly successful. Better still would be to purchase cassettes or records made by professional hypnotists, and study them for approach and voice tone, borrowing what seems to work and discarding the rest. By comparing my formula to other inductions you come in contact with, you'll develop one uniquely your own. The formula:

1. The subject is asked to sit or lie in a comfortable

position, preferably facing a wall or some other nondistracting surface.

2. He is asked to close his eyes and to take several deep breaths.

3. He is now asked to begin focusing his attention on his toes, their feelings and placement. Some hypnotists begin their induction on the toes, some on the forehead. There is no difference in the effectiveness of either method; it is solely a matter of preference.

4. He is instructed to imagine his toe muscles relaxing completely, more fully than ever before.

5. He is told to sense or feel that relaxation move into the balls of his feet, and the soothing sensation produced by such deep relaxation.

6. In a similar manner, he is asked to allow the relaxation to proceed through his arches, ankles, calves, thighs, hips, abdomen, chest, back, shoulders, neck, face and head. I pay particular attention to his back, shoulders and neck, incorporating imagery of restful massage and relaxation swirling through muscle groups.

7. When the entire body is covered in this manner, the client is told that he can continue to relax more comfortably and deeply by imagining the depth increasing with each count the hypnotist makes. The image of a stairway or escalator is commonly used here.

8. The hypnotist counts backwards slowly and regularly from ten to zero, pausing to suggest a deeper relaxation between each number.

9. Upon reaching zero, the subject is informed that he can now begin to notice the difference between this state and his usual awareness.

10. Hypnotic suggestions are now given and the subject is subsequently awakened.

The following is the PR induction version that I commonly use. Again, this is to act as a guideline, not a word-for-word system you should follow.

After I discuss the session's purpose with the client, and see that he is sitting comfortably in the reclining chair, I begin:

"Are you ready for some hypnosis? Good. Then get as comfortable as possible because you'll be in one position for awhile.

"All right, now, take a deep and relaxing breath, and because there is no reason to keep them open, you can allow your eyes to close. That's right. Another deep breath, and relax . . . breathing in relaxation, exhaling all unnecessary tension, letting every breath relax you more and more until I ask you to awaken.

"Each time you enter a state of hypnosis or self-hypnosis, you go into it more deeply than the previous time. Each time you go into hypnosis or self-hypnosis, you get better at it. And you can enjoy this time of deep physical and mental relaxation. You deserve a time to really relax.

"For the moment, now, concentrate your attention on your toes. Let your attention focus on your toes. You can allow the muscles in your toes to relax. Feel that sense of deep, soothing relaxation enter your toes. And your toes can relax.

"Now let that sense of relaxation move into the balls of your feet, so that the balls of your feet can easily, naturally, comfortably relax. And the balls of your feet can deeply relax.

"Now move that wonderful relaxation into your arches, so that your arches can share that sense of comfort and relaxation. And your arches can relax.

"Now let that relaxation move into your heels, and

around and up to your ankles. Your heels and ankles can enjoy that sense of relaxation, and relax.

"That relaxation can move up gently into your arches, easing in a peaceful feeling of comfort. And your arches can relax.

"Now that relaxation travels up, through each knee, and in and through both thighs. It may feel as if someone is pulling a warm and soothing blanket of relaxation up over your body, helping you to go deeper and deeper still, into this wonderful sense of tranquility. And your knees and thighs can relax, deeply.

"That relaxation travels up into your hips, and abdomen, and both your hips and abdomen can enjoy the benefits of deeply relaxing. And hips and abdomen can relax.

"Now that relaxation can swirl around into your lower back, easing in the most wonderful sense of comfort and peace. And your lower back can relax.

"That relaxation eases around into all the muscles of your chest, relaxing your chest muscles so much that breathing becomes easier. And your chest muscles can relax.

"Now that gentle sense of relaxation moves down both arms, to the elbows, to the wrists, and all the way to the fingertips, so that both arms can feel comfortably, easily relaxed.

"That relaxation now swirls around into your middle back, then flows smoothly up all the way to your shoulders, as though someone is giving you a gentle, pleasant massage. And all the muscles of your back and shoulders can relax, deeply.

"Now that relaxation travels up into your neck muscles, and the muscles of your neck can easily relax so much that your head can feel comfortably heavy.

"That wonderful relaxation can now swirl up into your

scalp muscles, so much that your hair can feel loose. And the muscles of your scalp relax.

"Now this relaxation travels down your face, relaxing your forehead, cheeks, and especially your jaw muscles. Your jaw muscles can relax so much that your teeth come slightly apart.

"And you can relax even more deeply than you have thought possible. Without realizing it, you have altered your breathing rate, you have increased your sense of relaxation. Without realizing it, you may already be entering the deeply relaxed state of hypnosis.

"Imagine yourself standing on a long and beautiful velvet stairway, leading down into deep and more comfortable relaxation. I'm going to count from 10 to zero and as I do, every number, every count will help you to move deeper and deeper, so that when I reach zero, you'll be in the deepest and most comfortable level of relaxation, going deeply into hypnosis.

"Starting down, now, ten. Relaxing more and more.

"Nine, going deeper and deeper.

"Eight, more and more comfortable, more and more relaxed.

"Seven, deeper and deeper.

"Six.

"Five, even deeper still.

"Four, further and further into relaxation.

"Three, deeply, deeply, deeper still.

"Twoooo, deeper.

"Onnnnnnne.

"And zero, deeper and deeper, relaxing more than ever before.

"The time you spend in hypnosis is a time of deep relaxation and revitalization. Every cell, every tissue, every muscle fiber benefits. Fifteen minutes in hypnosis is equal to an hour of deep and restful sleep in its benefits to body and mind. Later, when you awaken from this state, you will awaken feeling refreshed and alert, but now you can continue to relax, and enjoy this time for yourself.

"Notice the sensation in your legs. They may feel light or heavy, numb or tingly. This is the sign to you that you are actually experiencing hypnosis. And you can have this whenever you need it or want it.

"While you are in hypnosis, your control over yourself is magnified. You have amazing control over your body. You have skills and abilities you may have forgotten. Your memory is like a storehouse, from which you can retrieve any information. You are in complete control.

(give suggestions)

"And when these suggestions have been acceptable to your unconscious mind, you can slowly and agreeably bring yourself to full awakening, feeling refreshed, alert and wonderfully revitalized, knowing that you have done something very well."

Other Inductions

You may have noticed that the PR form I use is tailored to the kinesthetic person (see Chapter Two). Imaginative elements, such as "gentle massage," assist the right-brain individual more than the left-brain individual, but the induction also fits some other descriptions.

Inductions are "typed" as either *direct* or *indirect*. Each version has various descriptive terms attached, some of which are of old-fashioned usage. The direct induction form is also known to be literal, paternal, physical, dominant and demanding. The indirect induction is said to be symbolic, maternal, emotional, passive and suggestive. My induction could be called indirect, that is, delivered in such a way that the subject reacts to it as suggestion rather than a series of commands.

A direct induction would be delivered entirely differently, much like a stage entertainer would use it, for example:

"Close your eyes and take five deep breaths. Each breath takes you deeper and deeper into hypnosis. As you go into hypnotic relaxation, your body becomes relaxed and weightless. Soon you will be in a deep lethargic state."

Notice that the direct approach is more commanding, allowing the subject less opportunity to question or consciously doubt what is happening. Some hypnotists are suited by nature to a direct type of induction and can use it effectively and well.[1] You may consider using the direct form when you are familiar with the PR induction.

Traditionally, again, and within the framework of direct/indirect inductions, there is a further breakdown of methods of induction: fixation (fascination), levitation, monotony, imitation and rhythm. Modern techniques still make use of each of these, incorporating rhythm into the hypnotist's patter, as well as, occasionally, monotony. Levitation as used in the induction is more of a physiological phenomenon, much like the children's game of pushing bent arms against a door jamb, then stepping back to watch them rise "by themselves." The rock/balloon test is a part of the levitation procedure. Imitation, itself, is more a game of "pretend you can do this," such as relaxing deeply, but fixation and its relative fascination is the system most closely allied to the swinging watch approach—the eyes fixed unblinking on any bright or moving object produces optical fatigue and causes the subject to willingly close his eyes.

Inducing Hypnosis in the Visual/Auditory/Kinesthetic

Finally, given the principles covered in this chapter, the construction of an induction for the visual, auditory, or kinesthetic person becomes a simple matter of joining concepts.

With the idea that the PR form begins with relaxation of a small muscle group, then covers the entire body, an induction for the visual person might include:

"See the beautiful relaxation swirl up your calves."

"You inhale a deep, peaceful-blue breath of relaxation."

"You can picture a beautiful, sandy beach. See the warm afternoon sun sparkling on the waves."

Remember to bring in the visual person's secondary type, encouraging him to use his inner mind to a greater degree, such as following the beach scene above:

"Smell the fresh, salty air; feel the cool ocean breeze against your skin."

For the auditory person, focus on the restful sounds, including:

"Hear the regular, deep sound of your breathing."

"Really tune in to that inner harmony and relaxation."

Then bring in his secondary type as well.

To better understand the kinesthetic approach, you can review my induction and mark all the touch-oriented words. That will indicate how integral the kinesthetic focus is to that induction—and how difficult it would be to fit that version to a visual or auditory person.

When hypnotizing large groups of people, use an induction that equally incorporates all three types of awareness.

One point to consider is that, for those who are hypnotized very quickly, you should shorten your induction accordingly. An example will illustrate this: actors, actresses and creative people tend to be right-brained and imaginative—and easily hypnotized. I was supposed to hypnotize actor Anthony Hopkins on a movie set, and had only a few minutes to work. Still in costume, he sat in a dressing room chair. By the time I had suggested he take a deep breath and close his eyes, he was already showing numerous signs of hypnosis—including the eyelid flutter, breathing change and lack of swallow reflex. Noting this, I simply said, "Now you're in hypnosis," and went ahead. Within a minute, he was into an age regression, recalling a sporting event from his childhood! Interestingly, he said later that he had never been hypnotized before—but had been doing daily meditation for several years!

In summary, the whole concept of inducing hypnosis can be turned into a simple formula which consists of physical relaxation combined with a slow count from ten to zero. As you become more skilled, you will be able to ascertain how deeply each subject is into hypnosis by the time you are prepared to give suggestions.

Practicing alone will show you how to modulate your tone and tempo, although I suggest you experiment a few times with a tape recorder to understand the effects of a persuasive, encouraging voice.

The next chapter will provide the guidance you need to find your subject's level or depth of hypnosis, and where to go from there.

Notes to Chapter Four

1 Arnold Furst's *Post Hypnotic Instructions* (Wilshire Book Co., 1969) includes an excellent series of inductions and approaches to various hypnotic problems. The back of the book lists induction types for children through seniors. This work is invaluable for direct approaches.

CHAPTER FIVE

Deeper, Deeper: The Depths of Hypnosis

Hypnosis is a peculiar state; it is different from usual or normal awareness, but not so different that it is immediately identifiable as such. Yet, certain consistent phenomena occur in hypnosis (though not exclusively in the formal hypnotized state) that make the use of hypnotism very important in therapy.

Some of the conditions which can occur in hypnosis include age regression, amnesia, limb catalepsy (rigidity), aphasia (inability or unwillingness to speak), automatic movements, analgesia (absence of pain), anesthesia (absence of feeling), positive and negative hallucination, and catatonia (non-response). These can also happen without the induction of formal hypnosis, such as during an emergency situation or traditional therapy, but hypnosis is one of the few systems which can consistently *produce* the desired effects at *will*. The hypnotist no longer needs to wait for a "breakthrough" or catharsis for age regression to officially occur; he can help the client produce the desired state!

Any effect of hypnotism can happen at any "level" of the state—great depth is not required to produce results. However, by increasing the subject's depth—in other words, by increasing his focus on the situation under investigation—you can strengthen his ability to constructively use the appropriate skills.

For nearly half a century, various investigators have been trying to identify specific traits of the hypnotic state that would guarantee specific reactions from the hypnotized subject. Until fairly recently, these investigators did not understand that each subject will react only as is appropriate to himself, with just a few reactions common to all subjects. Attempts to create the perfect depth testing scale have continually failed for that reason. But, if depth testing is used as a general guideline and not as a demonstration of all specific reactions for all clients, then we can begin to agree on some traits as consistent at various levels.

General Depth Scale

There are three agreed-upon classifications used to identify the main levels of hypnosis. They are the Lethargic, the Cataleptic and the Somnambulistic.

Lethargy, or "light hypnosis": on the first induction, about 20 per cent of the general population is able to achieve this level. It is characterized by relaxation, eyelid catalepsy, catalepsy of isolated muscle groups, and a heavy or floating feeling.

Catalepsy, or "medium hypnosis": on the first induction about 60 per cent of the general population can achieve catalepsy. While the subject is in this state, he can experience complete muscle control, smell or taste changes, aphasia, amnesia, post-hypnotic analgesia, automatic rotor movements and partial hallucinations.

Somnambulism, or "deep hypnosis": for the first induction, 20 per cent of the general population can reach this level. Included in the results of this depth are positive auditory and visual hallucinations, bizarre post-hypnotic suggestion reactions, negative hallucinations, the plenary or comatose state via suggestion (the Esdaile State mentioned in Chapter One), and "trance logic."

Trance logic requires a detailed description,[1] for it is on this complex alteration of the subject's belief systems that much of modern hypnosis hinges. Many investigators feel that trance logic is the only way to truly distinguish "real" hypnosis from simple task motivation, the accomplishment of a given instruction.

Trance logic is the unusual and diffuse system of thinking used by the deeply hypnotized individual, and which is best described by example: A hypnotized subject believes he can speak only German. When asked repeatedly in complex English sentences whether he understands English or not, he answers negatively in German. He demonstrates that he *does* understand, even though he denies it!

A person not hypnotized, or faking hypnosis for test purposes (a "simulator"), will recognize the illogic of such a situation, and not perpetrate it. The simulator always reacts with conventional logic.

This means that the deeply hypnotized person—and, as T.X. Barber asserts (see Chapter One), some others—can assess information on at least two levels of understanding, but makes no attempt to correlate the facts. In other words, he can hold two conflicting beliefs simultaneously—his own and the one suggested by the hypnotist! And, after the hypnosis, the subject is able to rationalize whatever behavior he carries out.

Depth Testing

Depth testing in hypnosis is something like taste-testing foods: the hard and fast divisions are difficult to find. This type of work, then, has both its objective and subjective components.

Objective: This system is designed for the benefit of the observer or hypnotist. It can provide a reasonably reliable means of determining what phenomena your subject can experience at any given time in hypnosis.

A. Test for the Lethargic state: Both of the following tests will indicate whether your subject has achieved the light state of hypnosis. It is always wise to begin depth testing with the simplest tests before moving on to more complex ones.

1. Eye-closure[2]: the subject is asked to close his eyes and imagine, in whatever manner is natural for him, that his eyelids are becoming so relaxed that they simply will not work. When he is certain they will not work, he can test them—testing not to see that they *will* work, but that they *won't*. This is called a catalepsy of the eyelids. This test is one of the easiest with which to produce successful results.

2. Arm Catalepsy: To perform this test, your subject should already be in an apparent state of hypnosis, or have completed the eye-closure test successfully. You ask the subject to extend his right (or left) arm, and to imagine it becoming as stiff and rigid as a bar of steel. As you lightly touch each muscle group at the shoulder, upper arm and forearm, repeat that it is becoming like a bar of steel. You will notice with good subjects that the muscles visibly tense or contract. Then you may say that "in a moment, when I *try* to bend the arm, it will get stronger and stronger, so

that the harder I try to bend it, the stronger it will become." Next, you should make a good effort to bend the arm at the elbow. The instructions you've given are actually explicit enough so that, simply by doing what you suggest, the subject should produce the expected results. You may even be surprised at the subject's strength. When this test is completed, ALWAYS tell the subject that his arm is returning completely to normal, and be certain that it relaxes completely. Having accomplished these tests, your subject is in at least the Lethargic state of hypnosis.

B. Test for the Cataleptic state: After taking this test successfully, your subject should be able to perform any of the feats of the Lethargic or Cataleptic states. This test is for "glove anesthesia"—so named because of the numbness created in one hand. There are numerous ways to produce this response, each of which should be geared to the subject's representational system. The visual subject is asked to see a heavy leather glove being placed on one hand, and create a real picture from that idea. The kinesthetic or auditory person is asked to indicate with a finger move or verbally when that hand has begun to tingle and become numb. This test may take some time, and the subject should not have to strain or become tense to accomplish it. You may also consider the images of a bucket of cold, numbing water or of having novocaine in the hand—the content doesn't really make that much difference, as long as the idea of numbness in one hand is adhered to.

When the subject affirms that the hand "feels numb," and never before that, you may inform him that you will do the "pinch test" on the back of his hand, and that he will sense some pressure, but no discomfort. (Don't say "pain.") Then take a good hold on the skin, twist and pinch. You may wish to do the same to the back of the other hand, explaining that it is to show him that there is an appreciable difference. Remember to tell the subject that his hand can return completely to normal in every way at the conclusion of this test.

C. Test for the Somnambulistic state: Theoretically, by passing the following test, your subject should be able to manifest any of the other signs or phenomena of hypnosis. Practically, this is not always the case, due to the differences in each hypnotized person. This test involves the hallucinatory abilities of your subject. While hypnotized he is asked to experience a positive hallucination—the presence of something that is not there. For example, you may suggest he see and speak to Santa Claus, hold an imaginary parrot, or hear a particular strain of music. The subject's apparent behavior will indicate how completely he is following these suggestions. It is interesting to note that this test is at the base of much of Gestalt Therapy[3], where the subject is told to "put your mother in that chair and talk with her." No formal induction is used, but results are produced, nevertheless. Remember to return everything to normal before ending this test.

Subjective: All subjective tests revolve around the subject's belief in hypnosis and his reactions to it. Encouragement ("You look like a good subject") produces a better result than discouragement ("Why are you so resistant?"), and so it is with the production of a specific depth.

A. The Yardstick. This test emphasizes the internal experience of depth assessment. It is accurate insofar as the subject believes his own responses. You ask the hypnotized subject to imagine a yardstick (or barometer or whatever) having graduations from 0 to 36. From 0 to 12 on this scale represents a light state of hypnosis; from 12 to 24 a medium state; and from 24 to 36 or beyond a deep hypnotic state. When you snap your fingers lightly, the subject is instructed that a number will pop into his head—the first number, not his analytical reaction to it. That number represents the depth he has achieved at that moment, based on his subjective understanding of his condition. After asking if the subject would like to go deeper, you need only count slowly from the first number he produced to the depth you'd like him to reach. Then, check the number again to be sure. Most people operate best at the medium level of hypnosis, but will accept the suggestion to go deeper.

B. 1 to 10. This system is very similar to the yardstick, but employs the idea of numbers running from one (lightest state) to ten (deepest level). Like the yardstick, the subject is told what the numbers represent, then is asked to assess his own level. This test has the added advantage of simplicity, but doesn't allow the great variety and subtlety of response the yardstick test can provide.

C. Ask. The common sense aspect of this approach can sometimes be undermined by the caution of the hypnotist. If you are worried that your subject will not know how to respond, your feelings will be transmitted to him by your tone, posture, breathing changes and so forth. I don't mean that you should ask your subject, "Are you deeply hypnotized now?" but you should request the information from him in such a way that he is "obligated" to respond appropriately. For example, "Are you ready to allow that right hand to float upward?" This sign of the cataleptic state of hypnosis will occur if he is ready—and won't if he isn't. This system does require your verbal skill and a certain amount of sincerity. You *expect* the subject to have the specific reaction, and that will assist in producing it.

In any depth testing, you will find better results if you clearly explain to the subject exactly what his reactions will be to each test. That is, you are preconditioning him to respond the way you wish. Naturally, this explanation should be made in such a way that the subject understands his role, without feeling that he is simply acting out your requests.

In summary, though there is little general agreement on what constitutes the various levels of hypnosis, there is a concurrence on the three basic states of lethargy, catalepsy and somnambulism. A hypnotized subject can respond appropriately and well at any level, but most work is done in the cataleptic or somnambulistic states. Testing will sometimes help you determine just how deep your subject has gone into hypnosis.

The next chapter deals with the heart of hypnosis: giving suggestions.

Notes to Chapter Five

1 *Hypnosis for the Seriously Curious* by Kenneth Bowers (Aronson, 1977) has a particularly detailed description of the trance logic in Chapter Six.

2 This test can continue into an induction, as suggested by Dave Elman (see Notes to Chapter One).

3 Gestalt Therapy, developed by Fritz Perls, is an approach to psychotherapy and analysis which relies on the individual's feelings, particularly stressing the importance of being in the "here-and-now." Portions of Gestalt formula is to deal with past people and problems in the here-and-now, thereby releasing repressed unconscious materials.

CHAPTER SIX

What to Say and How to Say It: Giving Hypnotic Suggestions

What is a hypnotic suggestion?

One good way to describe it is by explaining what it is *not*: a command, an order, something that *must* be done. A hypnotist can act as a guide only, not a tyrant. So, a hypnotic suggestion is virtually the same as any kind of suggestion—an offering, a proferred path, a verbal gift that can be used in whatever way the recipient desires. It is the manner of presentation that makes this present viable.

Each person experiences the hypnotic suggestion differently. Some need to be directed precisely, some can operate on subtle hints, and some can supply their own guidelines.

I emphasize letting the subject work out his own best direction, based loosely on your general suggestions. If you had a video recording of your subject's life, up to the moment he arrived at your office, you still could not fully understand his true feelings, aspirations and motives. By telling the subject what to do in no uncertain terms, you:

1. assume you know exactly what is best for him
2. allow him no responsibility for his own actions
3. foster a continuing sense of dependence.

Since one of the aims of hypnosis is to create a self-responsible being, your use of indirect, subject guided suggestion will be the most effective in achieving this. As you gain more experience, you'll find yourself promoting those "miraculous cures" as the result.

What follows in this chapter are methods and techniques of giving suggestions, which should, in all cases, be tempered by your subject's unconscious reactions.

Foundation Concepts

The verbalizing of suggestions is of utmost importance. The central idea of the suggestion, the hinted-at change, is conveyed primarily through language, so your skilled use of speech is central to success.

There are several basic concepts that underlie all suggestion-giving. These are sometimes expressed as the Laws of Suggestion:

The Law of Association: When a positive event is associated in the subject's mind with a present experience, that experience will take on positive connotations. Or, a negative thought can be meshed with a current event to produce negative connotations. The basic idea here is that the subject's personal comprehensions can be "grouped" or arranged by associating them with the appropriate material. This Law is the structure within which the useful concept of "anchoring" operates (covered later in this chapter).

The Law of Reversed Effect: Also called the Law of Suggestive Reversal, it is one of the most potent types of suggestion that can be given. The subject is advised that the harder he *tries* to do something, the less he is able to do it. This Law is the basis for the Rigid Arm Test that is detailed in Chapter Four. You can see the result of his Law in daily occurrences—*trying* to fall asleep, *trying* to diet. There is always an element of doubt involved when this Law is in operation.

The Law of Repetition: Sometimes known as the Law of Repetitive Action, this is the basis of habit. When any statement, thought or action is repeated in like circumstances, a habit is instituted. Behaviorists[1] call this a "conditioned response"—each time the outside conditions occur, the response is generated.

This Law of Repetition leads to the development of habit "patterns." Patterns can be compared to solid belief structures (see Chapter Two), repetitious behavior created out of past need and enforced in current situations.

RAPPORT

In any human interaction, there must be a degree of "togetherness" or mutual understanding. It is this "sharing of experience," or rapport, that makes much of hypnotic work so satisfying. When your subject trusts you enough to relate his personal, painful, or joyous experience, he has found you to be trust *worthy*, a valuable compliment. To maintain rapport with your clients, you do not judge, criticize or belittle his motives or actions; you simply allow his experiences to be his own.

There are several useful techniques to assist in the process of developing rapport. All of these involve "sharing" your subject's world to some degree, choosing to experience what he does for the moment.

Representational systems: The visual, auditory and kinesthetic approaches as discussed in Chapter Two. This is the most direct use of the language to ally yourself with your client. It brings an automatic psychological closeness—and tunes your thoughts more closely to delicate interactions with your subject that might not occur otherwise.

Mirroring: You can find this behavior enacted anywhere in personal encounters. In restaurants, watch as two friends seem to duplicate each other in posture, breathing rate, use of implements, voice tone and so forth. It is a largely unconscious way of maintaining rapport, simply doing subtly whatever your subject is doing. If he taps his finger, you do also; if he folds his hands, you follow; he breathes rapidly, so do you. You'll find yourself very involved with what he is saying, perhaps even using representational systems without being aware of it. And your client will sense a closeness with you that he may never have known with anyone else before, without knowing why. Very successful therapists, such as Virginia Satir[2] tend to be skilled at mirroring to an extraordinary degree.

Pacing and leading: Pacing is similar to mirroring, but makes use of different systems. For example, to pace a subject's breathing rate, you might slightly raise and lower a hand at the same speed; as he nervously taps a finger, you might pace your speech to his raps. Leading is a method of utilizing the subject's pacing behavior, and is nearly always used in conjunction with pacing. It involves "guiding" the subject by first pacing, then changing the pace subtly into whatever is desired. You will have "lead" him from one inner experience into another. When your lead is accepted, much in the same manner as any suggestion is accepted, the subject begins to make the personal adjustments necessary to attune to the change.

Bandler and Grinder find good results through pacing and leading, even with catatonic persons—they have reported cases where the catatonic individual has leapt to his feet and asked them to stop!

It will be worth the little effort it takes to experiment with each of these rapport techniques, simply to discover for yourself how powerful their effect can be.

The Semantics

We return again to the use of our language as a means of beneficial suggestion leading to change. I've heard it said somewhere that telepathy is the basis for any language—otherwise, how could any two people agree on concepts as general and ambiguous as "good" or "bad"? Perhaps our usual difficulties in communicating with each other stem from a lack of common definitions, or the inability to articulate precisely what we mean.

Direct suggestion: The most straightforward, literal approach, direct suggestion operates by telling the subject precisely what you want him to do. "Please close your eyes" is a direct suggestion. Its primary benefit lies in the absence of possible misunderstanding between hypnotist and subject. Its greatest drawback is in the subject's conscious ability to assess, question and refute the suggestion. For this reason, I prefer the use of direct suggestion as an "instructional" or "request" device, not as a portion of the work to be done.

Myths and metaphors: In indirect hypnotic suggestion, precision is of utmost importance, but a type of preciseness that eludes conscious attention. It is the precision of purposeful vagueness, the speaking in broad, general concepts aimed toward a very specific point.

Both myths and metaphors are elegantly generalized systems of making a point, or giving a suggestion. Bruno Bettelheim's[3] work has established a greater significance for fables and mythology than had been previously realized.

Myths speak largely to unconscious processes, relying on an "innate" understanding of archetypes, those symbols common to a culture or to humanity as a whole. We unconsciously find major archetypes—the wise old man, the earth mother, angels and demons—occuring in our dreams, providing an intuitive awareness of occurring processes, as well as reaching into our emotional structures with support or criticism.

The use of fairy tales illustrates, by the use of archetypes (heroes and villains), exactly what is culturally expected of each child. Similarly, a well prepared anecdote or metaphor can produce the desired response in an adult.

Following are several examples of anecdotal metaphors. As you read through these slowly, notice your inner, emotional reactions. You'll note, too, that I have set them down like long poems. While I make no special claim to poetic skills, it is already known that poetry can open a door to the unconscious,[4] and in the pauses and silences between lines and thoughts, the inner mind forms its own vital and useful connections:

The USSR gave the US
a large polar bear
which was to be kept
at the Los Angeles zoo.
A special, natural enclosure
was to be built
for the bear
with ice-floes,
and chilled water

to fill his needs
exactly.
But while the new enclosure
was being constructed
the polar bear was penned
in a 12′ by 12′ cage
where he would pace
back and forth
all the time
12′ back and 12′ forth.
Finally the big day came:
polar bear and cage
were brought into the new surroundings
and I watched the cage door open
and the bear look out
at his new world.
Then he stepped out
and the cage was removed.
But I saw him
pace 12′ back
and 12′ forth.

One client of mine wept freely after hearing this while hypnotized. She said, "I know just how that bear felt—I've been doing the same thing myself." Unconsciously, she understood this metaphor, and identified with the caged bear, its eagerness to break from its confinement and its inability to do so even when the opportunity presented itself.

Another example indirectly asks the subject to compare past with present and discover the differences:

I was away at school for a year
and returned home that summer.
I was surprised

at how much smaller
my parents were,
how the chairs had shrunk
and the sink
I had once strained upward to use
I now tower over.

A direct suggestion which asked for the same response would be too demanding and technical for most subjects, and would require too much conscious, rational thought. Remember that this acts as a vague, general suggestion, too, allowing the unconscious mind to apply the process to *any* area of personal growth. The implication, however, is that change does occur with the passage of time; change that may not be perceptible until comparisons are made. There is also an implied suggestion to draw certain conclusions, and to notice the alterations with pleasant surprise and recognition.

Semantic "confusion": Allied with anecdotes and metaphors are the "semantic confusions"—juxtapositions of words that create a suddenly different and hence remarkable meaning:

You are opening a present
you see the present
touch the present
unfold the present
hear the present
and the past doesn't matter anymore.

Or:

Watch the bee flying
from flower to flower
and notice that

bee free-
ly flies.

—with the emphasis on "be free." In both cases, the unconscious mind adjusts to the leading thought, then must readjust its entire understanding of what has been said (that is, "present" as *gift* to "present" as *this moment*). There is an accompanying, and sometimes literal, burst of comprehension that follows this suggestion form.

Even Freud, whose main body of work has come under much fire, is recognized as the authority on this type of unconscious slip—the "Freudian slip." Example after example could be given (and here I refer you to Milton Erickson's work for thousands of fine examples), but the full power of this technique must be seen to be appreciated.

When you begin to use metaphors and semantic confusion you may feel very awkward. Most professionals in this culture have had to train themselves away from these right-brain activities during the schooling process. Yet the vast majority of our populace does not have the benefit of years of rational left-brain educations. Let yourself go into hypnosis (Gestalt therapy's equivalent "here and now," and the "uptime" of Bandler and Grinder), and the stories will flow easily.

Here are some usable ideas, general enough to be applied to non-specific life situations. You can make them fit your subject by adding personalized details.

1. A traveller on a long, arduous journey encounters many difficulties before reaching his/her destination.

2. A growing flower taking in vital nutrients from its surroundings.

3. Encountering difficulties in learning how to walk; ends by walking and even running taken as an everyday occurrence.

Again, these are to be used as anecdotes, metaphors, or

simply stories which illustrate or emphasize a specific point. For example, to one subject the growing flower may symbolize "growth" or self-support, using whatever "nutrients" or skills are available. When using this type of analogy, I would give the flower (or other figure central to the talk) the same gender as my subject and accent the words or concepts which are important.

You should note, when using myths and metaphors, that the subject's unconscious mind will use the material in whatever way is to his best interest. Consequently, any response is a good one. Don't expect your client to react in a specific fashion to indirect suggestion; his mind knows what is important to him. If the response that occurs is not what you both had in mind, use a different approach—don't keep battering away with something that doesn't work.

One client of mine, a young, painfully thin and shy man, seemed to react well to the "growing flower" suggestion. I had hoped to encourage use of his considerable talents by indirectly describing to his hypnotized mind how that "flower grows stronger every day, using his roots to pull in the important nutrients necessary for growth." His response during the next week was not what I would have expected, but kept fully within the bounds of the suggestion: he began to eat more, and of "organic" foods! When I changed the "growing flower" into an "opening flower in the warm, inviting sun" image, he then took more interest in using his skills.

Interspersal technique: When you listen to someone speaking you do not hear every word he or she says—you only perceive the words, ideas and pauses that are *emphasized.* Like the semantic approaches, the interspersal technique uses spoken language as its base, but it is the carefully worded emphasis on key phrases and ideas that gives it its strength. In the example following, notice how the accentuated portions contribute to their own kind of whole:

"It can be *very relaxing* just to think about the ocean . . . how the waves *drift* in and out *slowly*, and the *deep* blue water so *restfully eases* in toward the *ready* shoreline. Seagulls fly with a kind of *easy* assurance, so *calm* and steady in their flight, high and *low*, sometimes diving *deeply* into the *relaxing* sea."

Here, discussion of the beach leads the subject into a sense of calm relaxation, and an apparently senseless dissertation on suntanning ("warm sun makes me *feel so sleepy*") could continue the suggestion.

Use of the negative: "Don't bother trying to really understand this, because I know you can't." The subject reacts with shock: "Did the hypnotist really say that?" Then, anger: "I can't, eh? We'll see about that!" Finally, he accomplishes the negatively presented goal: "See, I really could understand!" And the hypnotist is forced to admit his error.

The key to using negative terminology is the basis of the dare: I'll bet you can't do this. Even in situations where the subject is suffering from severe apathy, the threat of being thought of as less than he is can be enough to get him started.

Somewhere at the very heart of using negatives is the Eastern philosophy of "the path of least resistance." Many clients will arrive for hypnosis hostile, angry, defensive and afraid. Trying to calm this subject, to remove his defenses or hostility will amount to practically nothing. Using his fear ("You're really afraid of me, aren't you?") will simplify your work tremendously by bringing him in immediate contact with his feelings, which opens him up to beneficial change.

I recall, as a tiny pre-schooler, seeing my first artichoke. Mother was sitting directly to my left, separating the leaves. I remember eyeing this strange object with suspicion. Was I supposed to eat that thing? Mother must have noticed my reactions. "Don't worry," she said. "You won't like it, so you're not getting any." I felt confused and angry—how did she know for certain I wouldn't like it? I gingerly sampled a piece, as Mother watched, stony-faced. Then I finished the entire thing off. To this day, I continue to eat artichokes with sublime delight: See, Mom, I proved you were wrong!

The double bind: Recent psychoanalytic work has demonstrated that the double bind command may be the generating factor in schizophrenia—experiencing two equally undesirable or exclusive alternatives in a given situation. Rational thought can find sieve-like holes in double bind reasoning, but the unconscious mind will work with the problem as given.

If I state to a prospective client, "Would you like to go into hypnosis in this room or in that one over there?", I have provided a bind. "Go into hypnosis" is taken for granted, but he is given the choice of where. When that decision is made, it is automatically assumed that hypnotism will follow.

Similarly, any two *apparently* opposing alternatives can constitute a double bind:

"You can go into light hypnosis today, or deep hypnosis."

"Will you notice the change by five o'clock today or by Tuesday?"

"If your unconscious mind wants you to go into hypnosis, your right hand will raise, otherwise your left hand will (eliciting hypnotic phenomena either way)."

But because double bind material is so near usual, conscious awareness, you must present it with as great a sense of confidence as possible. The assurance in your voice, coupled with the subject's desire to accomplish the given goal, is often sufficient to make the double bind especially effective.

Pattern interruption: Any stimuli which alters or arrests a habit pattern is known as "pattern interruption." For example, one pattern may be fear at the thought of leaving one's home. The pattern interruption may be a sudden house fire, where the individual leaves the home under a impetus stronger than the previous fear. In the therapeutic setting, any pattern can be interrupted by unexpected behavior on the hypnotist's part, or by interjection of an anchor (covered later). The hypnotist can hiss, clap his hands, point or look over the client's shoulder, and so forth, any of which will interfere with the patterned behavior.

During the process of pattern interruption, the subject's mind momentarily switches off the previous track and runs in a "holding pattern." At this point, I like to paraphrase Erickson with, "How surprised will you be when that habit is gone?" That will click the subject's mind to the projected thought of the problem he is resolving, and you can watch his eyes move to his right (as in Chapter Two). His answer of "Very surprised!" presupposes that he now expects the change to take place, and that he will be very surprised when it does!

Pattern interruption can be used at any time an unwanted pattern is discovered, but keep in mind that it will not eliminate a habit pattern—only disrupt it temporarily until other suggestions take effect.

Projection: A hypnotized woman begins breathing in a labored fashion. I ask her what she is feeling.

"An emptyness," she answers. "Like a void in my chest."

I ask her to describe the void.

"A great cold, swirling grey cloud."

She is not seeing a physical "reality," but rather an emotional one, landscaped and colored to match her personal symbolism. I wonder if seeing it from a distance would change its quality for her.

"Breathing normally," I say, "exhale that cloud until all of it is across the room."

She seems to focus on her breathing. Her eyes move under closed lids.

"Is it all across the room now?"

"Yes," she states.

"Is it different over there?"

"Smaller."

Good, I think. Something becomes less important when at a distance. Now, let's find out just what this emptiness means. I ask her to "watch this cloud very closely. It may begin to change into something that has special meaning to you. It may be a landscape, a portrait, a sensation. What's happening?"

She appears to watch, mentally, for a moment. Then, "Oh! It's my mother's face!"

"And what sort of expression is Mother wearing?"

A pause. "She's intent . . . staring at me . . . angry . . . or disapproving."

We've got it, I think. A few more connections like this one and this woman will realize her sense of emptiness stems from her childhood reactions to Mother's disapproval. I variously have her watch Mother's lips for words, hear sounds, or watch what Mother does next. Certainly, though it now is obvious to me that her "void" and "mother" are related, I do not make that statement. Her unconscious mind will make the right connections at the right time.

It becomes remarkably apparent that the unconscious has its own system of associations and joinings, just like this one. The conscious mind, however, may not be prepared to "learn" these inner truths. So, with this technique, the unconscious process is projected outward—where the client can feel safe to deal with it—and viewed objectively in another representational system, one of the subject's own choosing.

The client may experience a revelation as the conscious mind makes the necessary connections, and then realize that he really "knew" it all along but just didn't want to face facts.

This particular approach can be used with any symbolic material. Simply suggest that the client project the symbol and then deal with it. I've even used this method to eliminate tension headaches: visualizing the sensation as an object, usually a dark, fuzzy sphere, and watching it roll out a door and away.

Anchoring

This remarkable phenomenon derives its strength from the Law of Association, discussed early in this chapter. Part of anchoring's beauty comes from its simplicity; part comes from its amazing effectiveness, when used intelligently.

The unconscious mind, as part of its overall work, forms associations, combining disparate "events" into a single, cohesive whole. Jane Roberts writes of such a synchronization while listening to a radio symphony:

> The music boomed out. A flock of pigeons came to the roof. They pecked at the birdfeed in rhythm to the music so that paper, birds and me were all caught in the same motion, responding. Another crescendo now. Yes, the birds all flew away together. Was this all my own organization?[5]

For our purposes, we answer her question by stating that the organization of pigeons and music *exists*, that some part of that author's mind joined the events in just such a precise manner that they became a whole.

Anchoring is essentially the same thing. The subject's separate "events" of an emotional reaction are associated with your touch, sound or gesture. It is a conditioned response, strengthened by repetition. An example will help to clarify this:

I am hypnotizing a woman for the first time. After she has demonstrated specific hypnotic behavior, I say, "You can have this state of relaxation whenever you want it," while lightly touching the back of one of her hands. After that, each time I touch the back of that hand in the same spot, I notice she takes a deep breath and appears to relax more deeply. In the future, when I wish to hypnotize this woman, I ask her to find a comfortable position, then touch her hand in the same way.

Basically, her unconscious mind has associated that gentle touch with deep relaxation. Every time I reproduce that initiating touch, her mind associates it with relaxation.

Kinesthetic anchoring is not the only system that can be used. A certain tone of voice you use when doing hypnosis can be an anchor, and the special "hypnotic" stare some people expect you to have can also be an anchor. Any married couple will show numerous anchors: the raised eyebrow that precedes an argument, the tone of voice that starts the tears, the special hug that makes everything all right.

Furthermore, one anchor can be used to nullify or offset another. The power of this can best be expressed by watching it happen. If you anchor a subject's right hand by touch, using the idea of "feeling good about yourself" (in all three representational systems: "see yourself standing," "how does your voice sound," "feel that good feeling"), then anchor the left hand with "feeling bad about yourself," and finally apply both anchors simultaneously, you'll bring about an insightful experience. Your subject will evidence an amazing series of inner reactions, reflected unconsciously in muscle tension, pupillary changes, movement of the lower lip, skin texture, and color changes. You should hold both anchors until the subject has "finished" his coordinating; he may suddenly smile, become very calm, or cry happily. And he will feel very good about himself, without knowing why.

You will have provided a direct confrontation in that subject's mind between "good me" and "bad me." For some unknown reason, he will end up feeling either good or neutral, never bad. His inner mind will have contrasted all parts of himself associated with both feelings, meshed them, and produced a result beneficial to his whole person; and this in a space of less than *three minutes*.

Anchors can be used to simplify and speed up all therapeutic work, to gain access to specific material, or to produce a desired response. You can anchor specific behavior for later reproduction ("Show me how you would like to act in that situation, or how someone you respect would act"), or when there are rigid or repetitive behaviors you wish to interrupt. In that case, the negative behavior is anchored to something unpleasant.

Bandler and Grinder[6] describe anchoring the image of a rattlesnake crossing the floor to one couple's arguing: each time the couple began to disagree, the hypnotist stared at the floor as if following the imaginary snake across the room. The couple stopped within a half hour!

If you wish your subject to know what you are doing with your anchors, place the anchor in his representational system. If you wish the anchor to be between you and your subject's unconscious, anchor outside of his representational system.

The limits to anchoring are strictly those you impose; much experimental work remains to be done in this field. Consequently, you may feel free to use anchors in conjunction with every area of hypnotism.

A Formula for Suggestion

Having an understanding of how to present a suggestion is only a portion of the art. To be truly effective, that suggestion needs to be given in a specific fashion, a system that allows for the unconscious activity and interplay of the subject's mind.

The formula which follows is called "reframing."[7] It is best used after you have achieved some degree of rapport with the subject. For the average client, I will use this approach only after noticing the subject's willingness to change, as evidenced by his reactions to metaphorical commentary about personal growth.

1. *Define the problem:* This first step may seem fundamental, but it is often the step which is overlooked or taken for granted. The client who wishes to lose weight may or may not be suffering simply from overactive taste buds. "Losing weight," then, may only be a portion of the situation (as covered more fully in Chapter Ten). Spend some time discussing the problem with the subject, so that you are certain you both are aiming for the same goal.

2. *Identify the specific pattern to be changed:* You will be looking here for the *process*, or way in which the pattern is carried out, rather than the *content*. If the person is terrified of cats, the content is "cats make me afraid;" the process is "something frightens me"—a subtle but important difference. That process is the pattern to be changed.

3. *Establish a line of communication with the "part" responsible for the pattern:* Ask the subject to make a di-

vision in his behavior, designating the portion creating the pattern as an errant "part" or portion of the psyche. Ask that part if it is willing to communicate with you. Notice how it replies, whether it is by unconscious signal, verbally, or a combination. Any reply here is an excellent sign. Don't make the mistake of assuming the response must follow a specific pattern; let it operate on its own. Let the subject tell you whether the reply is "yes" or "no", and use that yes/no system for the rest of the session.

If the part is not willing to communicate, use an approach that goes something like: "Well, I wouldn't want to talk to someone who was trying to destroy me either. Go inside and apologize to that part." Give the part credit for having worked so hard in the face of so much conscious resistance. Ally yourself with it, and you will get better communication. If one approach doesn't work, use another and another until it does.

4. *Ask the intention of the part responsible for the behavior:* Here you can expect verbal as well as unconscious replies. As long as the subject learns what the intention is, whether he tells you or not, it's not necessary for you to know. Intentions may vary from obvious to unusual, but it's not your job to judge.

5. *Thank the part for having done such a good job in the past:* This, too, is important. That part, just like anything that does it's job consistently, "wants" to be appreciated. Remind the part that its actions have been for the good of the whole person. Ask that part if it would really like to be appreciated for its beneficial efforts. Wait for a "yes" answer.

6. *Create new alternative(s) to satisfy the part's intention, and aid the whole person in a constructive way.* In other words, ask the subject's "creative" part to develop at least three new ways of behaving in the problem situation. Or if the subject is not creatively oriented, ask the "plan-

ning" part, or the "devious" part to go to work—and to indicate when that work has been done. It is not necessary for either you or the subject to know the new behaviors consciously. You may ask the unconscious mind for a signal of completion: a raised finger, a nod of the head, having the eyes open, etc.

7. *Ask the part originating the problem if it is willing to be responsible for using the new behaviors in the appropriate situation:* A "yes" answer sends you to the next step. A "no" answer indicates you've done something wrong. Either go back to the previous step, ask the part "Why not?" and act accordingly, or have the devious part go to work to make it acceptable.

8. *Ask if there are any other parts that object to the new alternatives:* If so, take each of those parts back to step 3. If not, the reframing is complete.

Keep in mind that each part may answer in its own unique way. One woman saw various shades of purple, which diminished or deepened, as her "yes/no" signal. Another client signalled by twitching his toes, and wasn't even consciously aware of it. This is another type of unconscious communication, the "ideomotor" signal. You may also choose to assign a specific signal to a certain movement—for example, raising of right index finger for "yes," left index finger for "no." Often, as a variation of anchoring, I will very lightly touch a client's finger while stating, "Your unconscious mind knows how to show me when it is finished." The finger will twitch or raise at the appropriate moment.

Creating a "New" Past

In some instances, the subject does not have past examples of the new desired behavior to draw upon. Further work may be necessary to "provide" those past experiences, even as imaginative or fantasy material. Remember, the unconscious does not have the capacity to determine the veracity of information it accepts.

You can use direct suggestion effectively at this point by asking the subject to "imagine yourself really saying those important things to your boss last year," or whatever.

If the problem has been a long-standing one, such as an overweight condition originating in childhood, you may need to include "new past" actions the subject may not have been exposed to before. This could include athletic participation, admiration from a childhood member of the opposite sex, experiences of not wanting to eat when tired after play, and so forth. You can easily draw on your own experiences here—skating, running, jumping, being picked for baseball captain—to guide your suggestions.

Where there is a habitual physical pattern, such as in long-term smokers, you may wish to transfer that pattern into some other useful skill: writing, knitting, painting, etc.

Both you and your subject will always realize that part of his "past" was created as a therapeutic measure; there is little or no chance that the subject will entirely reject his real past in favor of the conjured one.

To summarize, when giving hypnotic suggestion, make it a point to begin each session with the development of rapport, through pacing and mirroring, and by a general discussion of the subject's life. In my experience, most clients only open up fully at about the third session, so I don't press for details or information outside the scope of each session.

It is implied in this chapter that the subject will present the reasons for each session himself, if you are perceptive enough to recognize what he is trying to convey.

When using metaphorical material, I generally find it makes excellent preparatory guides for the subject's unconscious activity—restructuring his patterns, if you wish. It is exceptionally gentle and consequently gets outstanding results.

Reframing, on the other hand, is the active work of hypnosis, though with a receptive subject a formal hypnotic state isn't even necessary. Following the steps outlined gets remarkably quick and lasting results.

But it is in the development of a "new" past that I really let my own creative part enjoy itself. Not all clients require this type of approach, but of those who do, many will spontaneously join in the fun and devise further details!

All in all, as you begin to practice with hypnotic suggestions, you'll find that it is hard—very, very hard—to say the right thing at the right time. You'll always think of something better afterwards. Let me briefly suggest that you let your own inner voice, or images, or feelings, guide you. That amazing unconscious mind just might know a lot more than you consciously think it does!

How much more that inner mind knows will become evident in the next chapter.

Notes to Chapter Six

1 Behaviorists contend that most if not all human actions are the result of conditioning provided by the individual's early experiences and environment. Activity is considered a conditioned response to stimuli, not the result of rational planning or "higher" thought.

2 Virginia Satir is a family therapist who has gained an outstanding reputation due to the success of her work.

3 Bruno Bettelheim's book, *The Uses of Enchantment* (Knopf, 1976), will be an excellent introduction to mythology as a teaching device.

4 *Poetry the Healer*, edited by Jack J. Leedy, M.D., (Lippin-

cott, 1973) carries some remarkable examples.

5 In her *Psychic Politics*, (Prentice-Hall, 1976), page 159.

6 *Frogs into Princes*, (Real People Press, 1979).

7 Reframing was initially developed, I believe, by Bandler and Grinder, although I have seen it used by various therapists under different names.

CHAPTER SEVEN

Looking Backward and Further: Age Regression in Hypnosis

Gradually and without much finesse we are beginning to comprehend the vast potentials of our own minds. Fifty years ago, who would have thought it possible to recall—actually relive—events of a long-forgotten childhood? That birth could be viewed through the eyes of the baby? Or that profound amnesias could be pierced in a matter of minutes?

Yet, hypnotic age regression does that, and more, on a regular basis today. This "regression" is an actual, evidenced mental "return" to a past event in the subject's life. It can come as a memory, or as a startling revelation; encouraged or unbidden. Formal hypnosis has made age regression a respectable part of psychoanalysis, medicine and the law.

In the mentioned professional circles, regression is used

to release repressed unconscious material—therapeutically and in legal matters. As with any function of the mind, of course, material which the individual does not wish to deal with will remain repressed, so there is no chance of regression being used against someone's will. Hypnosis cannot be used to make a criminal confess, for example. A person can lie while hypnotized, or produce elaborate fantasies on the innocent instructions of the hypnotist.

There continues to be a controversy over the use of regression in police procedures to assist eyewitnesses to crimes in recalling pertinent details. Some authorities believe that even the slightest hints or "leads" from the hypnotist can cause the subject to veer from the memory he had of the witnessed crime into an inaccurate version.[1] It is certainly possible for this to happen, but with proper technique the possibility can be avoided. "Leading" a subject is discussed in the recalled regression section.

But regression itself is not as simple as it may appear, nor is it as difficult to achieve as some would suggest. As with any phenomena of hypnotism, a common sense attitude discloses basic concepts.

The Theory

Each past event is connected to the present by what we call "memory." Memory is the individual's viewpoint of what occurred at a particular time and place. Any two people involved in one event may have entirely different memories of what happened; memory is fallible to the extent that it records only one perspective of the overall "reality."

The memory, as recorded in the unconscious mind at the time of the event, remains fixed and unchanging. The conscious portion of the memory alters dramatically through the passage of years.

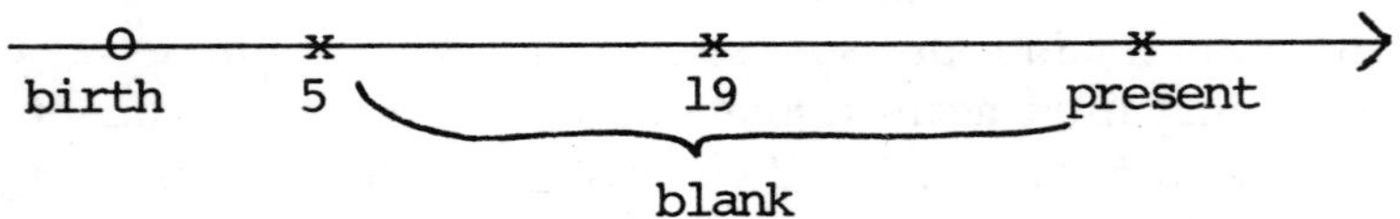

The event at age five is recalled or relived as if the subject were still five years old, the intervening years being "forgotten" or ignored.

For example, a childhood experience at the age of five, of being locked in a closet, is stored without change at that age on the time line. Consciously, the adult may recall the closet incident, may be able to laugh at the child's fears, or comment on the effectiveness of the punishment. However, during regression, the unconscious mind opens its storehouse and the vividness and immediacy of the five-year-old's perceptions are resurrected.

The regressed individual outwardly may take on the mannerisms, speech patterns and thoughts of the appropriate age. Some subjects will even have difficulty integrating the presence of the hypnotist into the "past" where the hypnotist did not exist.

On the other hand, the person in regression may retain some awareness of his current surroundings. Having regressed many times, to various ages, I can verify the astonishing sense of being a child again, mentally stepping into that tiny body—feeling, seeing and hearing things long past as vividly as if it were now happening—yet always knowing I was resting as an adult in a reclining chair and undergoing regression.

Experiments indicate that the subject mentally returns to the regressed age, making use of knowledge gained up to that time only. Hence, a 30-year-old regressed to age eight would have no "usable" memory of Watergate—simply because the Nixon era did not exist until he was twenty three. That memory lies somewhere "ahead" on his time line.

In theory, that is the concept we use in regression. In fact, the mind forgets nothing. If a subject is regressed, he still has a brain crammed full of years of learning which, for the moment, he chooses to ignore. Later in this chapter, you'll see how we can make use of this fact by having the "adult self" advise the past "child self."

Milton Erickson suggests that the only "true" regression is marked by an absolute dismissal of all information beyond the age regressed to. It is unfortunate that a hypnotist who has been instrumental in expanding the limits of hypnosis and exploring the mind's potential would get himself stuck on this one. Since the brain remains intact during regression, nothing prevents its use of its own circuitry in whatever manner it chooses . . . except the limiting beliefs of subject and hypnotist!

Regression itself may be used for a variety of reasons, but it is not the final or most successful approach to hypnotism. In many cases, reframing (Chapter Six) provides superior results. However, there is still a need in psychoanalytic circles, and in certain psyches, to see or undergo emotional release before healing can begin. Regression has been compared to draining an infected or pus-filled wound prior to stitching it up. Some hypnotists have carried on successful practices without ever doing formal regression. Again, as in most of hypnotism, what the unconscious minds involved (yours and the client's) believe is necessary will be. You may *have* to use regression on a "sophisticated patient"—one who has been through therapy before—because he won't accept personal change without a dramatic exposition of some sort.

Energy Concept

In a therapeutic setting, we can envision *regression* being used to counteract *repression*. In the following diagram, what has occurred and was repressed at age seven will remain as "stored energy" at that age, inaccessible to the present self.

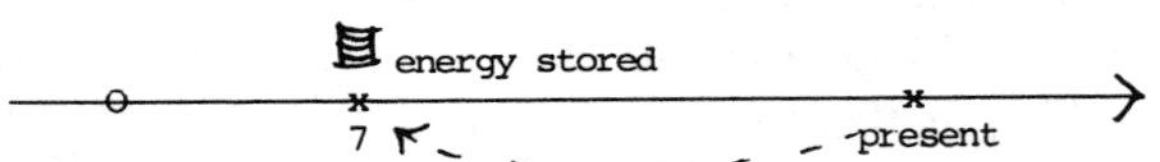

Energy stored at age seven was not available between seven and the present age. Regression can make that energy available in the present—but not to the intervening years.

The basic idea is that a specific "amount" of personal energy is used in or by the act of repression. With enough repression in process, much personal energy is tied up and hence not available for current use. You can find examples of this in many instances of neurotic or compulsive behavior, such as compulsive hand washing. The individual expends a given amount of energy in the repeated action. When the need for the action is removed, the same "quantity" of energy is now ready for other purposes.

Certainly, when we speak of "energy" here, we are using a very subjective approach. This personal energy may be creative in nature, it may be basic biological energy. It is not tangible, so we must deal with it as the intangible that it appears to be.

During age regression, the trapped energy becomes usable in the subject's present. Or, to put it another way, the energy which was used for repression is available for present use. In any case, successful therapeutic regression produces a psychological sense of freedom from previous restrictions.

Conduct of a Regression Session

Unconscious permission is a prerequisite to assisting your client in regression. Without that inner mind's okay, you may find yourself faced with a great deal of resistance or downright avoidance. With unconscious agreement, virtually anything can be done.

You can secure the inner mind's consent simply by asking for it—and being attentive to the many potential forms the reply may take. Then, follow the steps outlined in the diagram on the next page.

Giving Insight

"Insight" is the personal understanding of what occurred during regression. The insight, or comprehension of events, that a child may hold is quite different from what the same adult may support in later years.

After completing a regression, you may find it necessary to "explain" what happened in the past in a way that the adult's inner mind can comprehend. In many cases, this means taking the "child's side," and discussing what was done from that viewpoint. The following examples can indicate a generalized pattern where the given feelings come up in regression:

STEP ONE — Ask the hypnotized subject's unconscious mind if it will be all right to explore the problem.

STEP TWO

- **if YES** — use regression
- **if NO** — can the unconscious work on problem without exploring it?

STEP THREE

- abreaction — go thru event several times to "discharge" emotion. Give insight.
- recall — go thru event, give insight as required.
- if yes — instruct unconscious to work on problem.
- if no — work on at later time. End session.

IS THIS ACCEPTABLE TO THE UNCONSCIOUS?

IS THIS ACCEPTABLE TO THE UNCONSCIOUS?

Are there other events involved?

STEP FOUR

STEP FIVE

- **if YES** — go to step one
- **if NO** — is the explanation acceptable to the unconscious?

Therefore, it is no longer necessary to retain symptoms.

STEP SIX — Awaken subject.

Anger: "You were right to feel that way, after what happened to you. No one has any right to treat a child that way. Now that you are old enough to understand what they did, you can really see them as the unhappy people they were."

Grief: "You can understand that child's confusion and his feelings of loss—and know you really did survive, even when you thought you wouldn't. Saying goodbye is hard for a little one, but you have learned to say goodbye in peace."

Guilt: "You've suffered enough through the years to make up for that mistake."

Fear: "The things that frightened that child were all so much bigger than he was. They remained back there, but you grew up. You are much bigger now than you ever thought you could be, bigger than any of those bogeymen."

Remember, the aim of giving insight is not to eradicate the subject's past emotions. It is a way of helping him or her see past actions in a different and, hopefully, more mature light.

Recalled Regression

Grouped under the heading of age regression are various outward forms, each having unique characteristics which allow a certain leeway in classification. We divide regression on the basis of how it looks to the observer; the subject's experience can be compelling whether he shows it or not.

Recalled regression is essentially an encouraged memory. The hypnotized subject will speak and act as if he is remembering the event: "Then we went over to Aunty's house," or "He hit me. My head hurt."

Recalled material can be a gateway into an abreaction (covered shortly). It is, primarily, a method for remembering forgotten material—misplaced jewelry, witnessing of crimes, etc. As such, the emotional elements are not present to a strong degree.

After being hypnotized, the subject may be instructed to "watch a movie" of the incident or otherwise place some psychological distance between himself and the occurrence. A complete method for carrying out a regression follows in the portion on abreactions.

Leading: It is important that you avoid leading the subject during a recalled regression. Leading is that habit of asking questions which advance the action of a regression by offering alternative memories. "Are you going inside the house now?" is a leading question, and for some suggestible subjects it can act as an instruction: "Go inside the house." Either the subject will:

1. recall another instance, another time of going inside or
2. fantasize entering the house.

Leading is a sloppy hypnotic technique. It will also invalidate criminal proceedings, age regression experiments, and "past life" regressions. In these areas, the subject's own memories are what is paramount, not what the hypnotist supposes, hopes or suggests happened.

To reduce a tendency to lead the subject, use noncommittal phrases to advance the action in regression, such as, "What happened next?" "Something important happened next, what is it?" and so forth.

Abreaction

This is the most demonstrative form of regression. In an abreaction (also known as a relived, or revivified regression) the subject acts out each element of the past experience. This can be used therapeutically to release repressed energies and memories. The dramatic strength of this abreactive release is called a "catharsis;" much psychotherapy is aimed toward bringing about catharsis. It can occur without hypnosis, but by using hypnotism the entire process is sped up, sometimes saving years of analysis.

The subject should maintain verbal contact with you throughout the regression, describing or acting out his feelings and experiences. This simple monitoring system is your way of knowing exactly what is happening.

After the regression, the subject should be encouraged to recall as much as his unconscious mind will let him. An arrangement can even be made with the unconscious to make memories available to the conscious mind at the rate it feels is best, using dreams or revelations. In general, regression is effective when there is some conscious acceptance of past issues. Where there is no conscious memory of a regression, it indicates the material or incident covered was too traumatic for the conscious to deal with.

Abreaction is one of the most difficult hypnotic procedures for the hypnotist to personally cope with. The subject will be generating a good deal of repressed energy: a 190-pound man screaming at the top of his lungs, pounding the arm chair he sits in or *your* desk, is a formidable sight. In his mind, he may be a six-year-old yelling at mom, but in your world he is an enraged powerhouse.

Consequently, you will need to be "on the subject's side" in his regression, identifying yourself to his unconscious as a friend, guide or his inner helpful voice. There are limits to that, though, too. You must not be so solicitous and comforting that you prevent the subject from experiencing his emotions. A subject who undergoes profound sobbing doesn't need to be cuddled—even though that may be *your* first reaction. He has a right to deal with his feelings in his own way—that is, by expressing them—and if you touch a person who is abreacting, you will most certainly anchor (Chapter Four) his experience to that touch!

The point of abreaction is to release trapped energy, and the reliving of the event, one or more times, does just that, as well as bringing the memory to conscious awareness. Therefore, the subject must re-experience the past emotion if regression is to do any therapeutic good. You must be willing to let him do so—without compromise or limit, but within reason. Generally speaking, since the client survived the revivified event once, he can do so again, but the severity of the abreaction will need to be monitored to some degree. It is difficult to set hard-and-fast rules on this since individual experience may vary so much.

I let the subject's physiological responses be my guideline. If the client is displaying emotion and the "normal" physical counterparts of that feeling—tears, anger, shouting, stamping his feet, hitting walls or furniture, etc.,—I want him to continue, sometimes even encouraging him to become more dramatic, more expressive. But if the client begins to show "abnormal" physical reactions, such as seizures, vomiting, "memory tissue," unusual changes in skin color, etc., I'll suggest a toning down of the abreaction into a recalled regression.

"Memory tissue" is a physiological phenomenon where the subject's body will actually reproduce—in moments—the texture and substance of a past wound or injury. A red, raw patch may appear where the client was burned as a child; it may even blister in the course of a few minutes. Other than the amazing ability to demonstrate this effect clinically or experimentally, there is no actual need for the subject to resuffer a physical injury. It will subside when the subject ends the regression, or on suggesting a recalled regression as replacement.

Yet, even that choice between normal/abnormal reactions is modified by the particular client. One woman in an abreaction first wept, then began convulsive spasms that were almost orgasmic in appearance. She commented on her feelings during the spasms, indicating that although there was some discomfort, they seemed to produce a tension release. She continued to have the reaction for nearly twenty minutes, then relaxed spontaneously. She phoned several days later to inform me that her muscles were sore, but her outlook had brightened and she felt happier and more creative. However, one man abreacted to surgery he had as a child, wept briefly, then progressed into rigid, full-body convulsive movements. His communications with me changed from those of a child to fearful moans. At that point, I suggested he switch to a recalled regression, and view the scene "from a safe distance." He did not consciously remember any details of the regression afterwards: the material was too frightening for him to deal with on a conscious level. So his own protective unconscious mind did the best thing possible—it kept the memory in repression.

As previously mentioned, a person in regression will appear to be at the age or time to which he has regressed. Motor coordination, speech and writing skills may be appropriate to the given age, but there can be a certain amount of overlap, for example, where physical skills are correct but verbal facility is at adult levels. It is not vital that all systems regress equally; that is not the purpose of age regression. What is important is the beneficial effect the subject receives from his abreaction. As far as that goes, there is always the possibility that abreactive material may be the product of fantasy, but if it can produce some change for the better in the individual, it doesn't matter where the material came from. Honesty, of course, is always preferable, but we are looking for results over historical data.

In abreaction, as differentiated from a recalled regression, the subject speaks as though the incident is happening "now." He will use the present tense: "I am walking," "He is hitting me." It is this single factor which sets abreactions apart from other forms of regression—the immediacy of it.

Assisting the subject in the production of an abreaction can be relatively simple or extremely difficult. It may occur spontaneously in the middle of an otherwise mundane session, or it may require an intense set of hypnotic instructions. In any case, you must remember that the subject's inner mind will let out whatever is important. You should not insist where there is obvious resistance.

Generating an abreaction is a matter of technique. I usually condition my client beforehand by telling him what to expect: the vivid, "I-am-thereness" of the experience, perhaps an emotional response, and a heavy emphasis on benefits to be gained by releasing trapped energies. This also effectively instructs him on how to behave in regression and structures his responses somewhat. I indicate that he may come out of hypnosis and the regression at any time, should it become too much—but in several thousand regressions I've assisted, no one ever has.

Next, I hypnotize the subject and obtain his unconscious permission to begin the regression. The abreaction itself can be instituted in several ways:

Directed: The subject is instructed to "go back to . . ." the appropriate age or incident, when a time or event is known. One 30-year-old woman wished to find out if a recently recalled memory of a childhood molestation was real or imaginary. She consciously thought the deed might have happened when she was ten years old. Already a highly conditioned subject, she was easily hypnotized. I suggested, "Your mind is like a storehouse. Everything you have ever experienced is stored accurately and completely in your mind and is available for review now or at any time you wish. I'm going to count from 30 back to 10. As I do, you'll move back in time, back in time so that when I reach 10, you'll be ten years old. Your unconscious mind will provide all the details of that time, all the information you wish to know from that important event. Going backward in time, 30 . . . 29 . . . 28 . . . — . . . 11 . . . 10. The number 10, the age of ten. Notice your surroundings . . ." (and other phrases to help her establish her location on the time line) ". . . and what's happening?"

At this point, I spoke to her in the present tense: "What's happening?" as opposed to "What happened?" In fact, during an abreaction one of the most potent ways to distract the subject is to speak in the past tense; he may even switch from abreaction to recalled regression as a result.

In abreaction, the woman entered a trailer belonging to the older man, was shown "cheesecake" photographs, and expressed a feeling that something wasn't right about what was happening. Suddenly, she found herself resisting a weight on her legs and, although she couldn't (or wouldn't) see her assailant, she had the feeling that she was struggling under him. She was able to escape relatively unscathed, but never told her parents about the adventure, insisting to her ten-year-old self that she had done nothing wrong.

When she awakened from the hypnosis, this woman still sensed the feeling of pressure on her legs; a sensation she had as an adult during intercourse. She was still not convinced that the event had taken place as she recalled it, but could not understand why the pressure persisted in her legs. She was lightly re-hypnotized and we agreed that her unconscious mind would reveal details at its own pace as she became able to deal with them.

Non-directive: In this abreaction the subject is simply

instructed to regress to a time *just prior* to the onset of the problem. The theory here is that the unconscious will pick the event most concerned with the production of the difficulty. It is, after all, what the client is in hypnosis for.

As example of this, a 29-year-old student of mine expressed an interest in eliminating her allergy to cats. Whenever she came in contact with cat hair, she broke out in itchy hives almost immediately. She didn't recall exactly when the allergy began.

In hypnosis, she was given the same general instructions as the woman in the previous case, but instead of being counted back through time, I suggested, "Your inner mind has its own time line, its own understanding of each event in your life, what caused it and what the outcome was. As you rest comfortably your unconscious mind can move back effortlessly through the years to *something important happening just before* you noticed you were allergic to cats; something important, and your unconscious knows how to point out to me just when it has found that something."

I waited for a finger signal. She gave it. Her closed eyelids fluttered, and without further suggestion she described sitting at the kitchen table with her mother and siblings discussing the disposition of the family's pregnant cat. Because she was going into lengthy and (I felt) unnecessary reprocessing of the entire dialogue, I asked "What happens next?" to advance the action.

Next she found herself carrying the cat and one new kitten to the local animal shelter. Confused and hurt that her kitty was being taken away by that institution, she silently vowed—in that child's mind—that she would make it impossible for her ever to harm a cat again.

With that revelation, she was brought out of hypnosis. She was able to rapidly review each of her intervening cat-contacts from the new perspective, giving herself the necessary insight, and decided that she *could* contact a cat with only the most loving intentions in mind. Therefore, her allergy, a method of *protecting cats from her,* was not needed any longer.

A cat was immediately procured and she was able to pet and handle it without a recurrence of symptoms. She also soon after acquired a cat as a pet for her children.

She was one of those "miracle cures" that happen with hypnosis. But there was no miracle to it—simply a sensible understanding of the force of a child's decision and the adult's ability to reverse it!

Hubbard (Dianetic) Approach

Scientology,[2] one of today's "now religions," has a system for releasing traumas which is essentially a regression technique. They call it auditing. It is ideally suited for the auditory person because of its heavy reliance on verbalized material.

Dianetics claims to be able to "clear" anyone of psychological impediments through this technique, so that all personal energy is available in the present. Such a person is supposedly able to do the miraculous. While this is not meant to be a treatise on Dianetics or Scientology, it is interesting to note that this technique is "not hypnosis" according to all their literature. For our purposes, we can use the approach without the philosophy.

The theory behind the Hubbard approach is that repetition of a key phrase will tune the subject into a past event where the phrase was initially used. This repeated phrase is used to unlock a memory. The subject's conscious or unconscious use of the repeated phrase is the product of his experience. That is, the phrase may appear in his usual speech, or as a conscious thought just prior to remembering the event. The memory in question is stored in the unconscious in such a way that the process of repetition releases or desensitizes it.

Five phrase patterns or commands comprise the system. Each "verbal command" acts as a guide for the subject, both in his past and present. When the phrase is repeated in regression, it will trigger the same emotions as it originally did. In other words, if the past event in question is angry, the subject will feel anger; an imprint which says "forget it" will produce forgetfulness. A command such as "get out," repeated, should therefore send the subject to another regression experience—it would "get him out" of that particular regression. Following are the command types and examples of each:

1. Ejection type	"get out," "don't come back," "stay away"
2. Retention type	"come back," "I can't go," "stay here"
3. Happening now type	"I'll get even," "everything happens at once"
4. Denial type	"getting nowhere," "I can't talk about it," "can't remember"
5. Reversal type	"can't go back now," "you're turned around"

The point is that the verbal expression continued to influence the subject from its first effect on him up to the present.

I use this technique when a client repeats any given phrase several times in near succession. For example, one man during the pre-hypnosis conversation expressed surprise at a turn of events with "I can't get over it." He was also having difficulty ending a particular habit. He was hypnotized, then asked to repeat, "I can't get over it."

After several repetitions, he changed the phrase to "I'll never get over it," then to "He won't get over it, this is serious." As I asked him to repeat each new phrase as it developed, his inner mind led him back to a childhood event. He'd undergone surgery for appendicitis, developed an infection and seemed to be failing. "This is serious," apparently had been spoken by a doctor somewhere within earshot and faithfully recorded in his unconscious mind as a command. Thereafter, each time something was "serious," his inner mind followed the command, "Don't get over it."

The subject subsequently repeated each aspect of the event "from the beginning to the end" while hypnotized. Each repetition of the event discharges or desensitizes the association. I watched for one of the signs of that catharsis—boredom, apathy, humor, sometimes anger—and when he yawned, I knew it was finished. He was awakened without further suggestions and was asked to think about what bearing this childhood event may have had on his present situation. The following week he reported in only long enough to say that he had ended the annoying habit and made several other adjustments in his life. He also mentioned that "I can't get over it" appeared to be a theme underlying several major current issues in his experience.

An approach such as this does show the amazing ability of the mind to solve its own problems when given the opportunity to do so.

Informal Regression

Where the subject is hesitant to discuss information or past life details with the hypnotist, this informal or "secret" regression works quite well. The subject's verbal contact is not a necessity, but in its place you must keep a very close watch on his unconscious processes.

With the subject in hypnosis, memories can be stimulated by association. Asking you to remember the smell of your first baseball glove, the feel of the leather, the sound of your fist hitting it, will set off a series of associated memories. In a similar manner, when the subject is instructed, "There was that little boy (girl), so long ago . . .", he (she) will automatically associate that with the only "long ago child" he or she knew well—himself or herself.

"You can watch that child, feeling those feelings, without his knowing that he is being watched." This is another instruction to the unconscious mind to notice itself as a child, from an adult point of view. Naturally, the "feeling those feelings" would be modified to each individual situation.

"And you can let him know you're from his future, there to tell him that he really does survive . . ." This is an assurance to the child within that everything will work out well in the end.

Because the regression process is not out in the open as in other types, your awareness of unconscious processes must be exceptional. An eyelid flutter when the subject is asked to "see that child" would be a good indication that his inner mind is doing just that. Again, conscious awareness on the part of the subject is not important here. I recall one woman whose chest heaved, nose turned red, and lower lip trembled on being reminded that "she did survive." But when asked what she felt was happening, she said, "I don't feel any different. Am I still hypnotized?" Indeed she was, and doing some important inner work!

"Past Lives" Therapy

This is perhaps the most controversial of approaches, yet many exponents seem to be getting results.[3]

A twenty-one-year-old lesbian woman complains of a series of nervous breakdowns which she believes are related to a particular lover. She wants to "stop thinking about her all the time," and to stop "feeling so guilty" about certain aspects of their relationship. She is hypnotized and I instruct her to "go back, all the way to the beginning, to the first time you met each other."

The year, this client says, is 1858. She is now a man, meeting a woman she recognizes as the current lover, but different: younger, thinner, with a different face and personality.

The relationship is a good one. They marry a few years later. Now taking on the speech patterns of a man, my client describes in detail his joy at the news of his wife's pregnancy, then, the horror of her difficult labor. The wife dies painfully in childbirth. The husband, my client, is shattered. "It is my fault," she exclaims. "I did this to her."

He was to live out the remainder of his life a widower, raising the child and feeling guilty for having "caused" his wife's death.

I instructed the subject to return to the present with a full and complete memory. I suggested that her unconscious could begin to understand the connections between then and now, that she would awaken with a new realization of her purposes.

She came out of hypnosis slowly, then said, "I know why I'm gay now . . . so I'll never be able to get her pregnant again." Several years have elapsed. She has made an excellent adjustment and does not see the former lover anymore. She hasn't had a breakdown since that time.

There are several theories for past-life age regression:

Fantasy: Thus far, I have worked with seven Mary Magdalens, two Edgar Allan Poes and three Egyptian Ra-tas. There can be little question that such a series of historic personages gracing my reclining chair is indeed remarkable—and hard to believe. Certainly, past life regression may be nothing more than fantasy material, particularly when historically important figures appear. Nevertheless, when a subject can act out, and hence reduce, his hostilities as Napoleon, there is no reason to stop him from doing so. If fantasy produces results, then encourage it!

However, the majority of people I've worked with have led mundane enough past lives: one as a farmer in the midwest, one as a very boring logging man, one as an unhappily cloistered nun, and one as a merchant during the Revolutionary War. The high point of one woman's entire past life was watching a neighbor's barn burn down. If it is fantasy material, the consensus of concentration appears to be on personal development, personal relationships and growth, rather than participation in historical events within the past life.

Gene memory: This is a recent theory, tied to the concept of ancestral memories being stored in the genes and passed on to succeeding generations along with eye color and shape of the feet, etc.

It is the most "scientific" theory, but in my opinion, also the least feasible. If we speak strictly of genes, then my client whose known ancestry was recorded for several generations back to a small fishing village in Finland could not have regressed to that Mexican town at the turn of the century. If it had been a fantasy, he gets no credit for imagination, either.

On the other hand, if the subject recalls details from his own family history, gene memory might be significant—as long as the information was not previously told to him by parents or relatives.

Reincarnation: This, of course, is the most difficult concept to deal with—it presupposes that people do live other lives in other places. Most of the criticism of this theory comes from those who simply do not accept reincarnation as plausible.

Theological questions aside, some respectable researchers have unearthed remarkable information which adds some credence to the past-life theory. Ian Stevenson, Ph.D., a noted psychologist, has made numerous studies of "responsive xenoglossy," the regressed subject's speaking in a language he would not ordinarily know in his waking state. Cases are discounted when the individual has had some prior knowledge, study or contact with speakers of the language, because of the possibility that some portion of his mind may have picked up the language without his conscious realization. Nevertheless, Stevenson's studies have turned up people who, when in past life regression, speak archaic versions of modern languages, such as the French spoken in the 1600's. Unlike modern French, the subject would probably not have heard that variation spoken on a television program or in the movies.

Similarly, when a subject retrieves place names, dates and family names, it provides interesting material for personal research. Unfortunately, most historical records are vague prior to the twentieth century, especially outside of the United States; some information is simply impossible to find. However, when a subject "relives" a life in the U.S., it can be a unique experience in detective work to check records, grave sites, and military journals for a possible reference to the "past-life" person.

Jeffery Iverson[4] writes of such a situation in several celebrated past life regressions, documented with historical facts. He is extremely fair in his assessment of the information received in regression—and openly questions information contrary to "known" history.

Since the validity of this theory rests solely on a question of faith in reincarnation, it is nearly impossible to present an argument pro or con. It remains a matter of faith.

Telepathy: Since Dr. J. B. Rhine began his research decades ago into the incidence of "mind reading" or telepathy in the general public, all but the most skeptical have acknowledged that some "force" outside of the usual five senses is in operation. As will be discussed in Chapter Eleven, hypnosis tends to increase or accentuate the success of extrasensory perceptions.

There is a possibility that the person under hypnosis, in a past life regression, is actually performing a feat of telepathy: reading the mind of a deceased person, as if it were his own.

This theory presupposes that telepathy does exist, that it can occur independent of, or outside of time, and that a subject instructed to age regress would choose to mind-read instead of regressing.

Because it is a convenient and relatively plausible explanation for past-life age-regression experiments, it has become a popular theory. Naturally, acceptance of this idea must go hand-in-hand with a much enlarged belief in mental functioning: if a hypnotized mind can pick up details of another person's life, perhaps it can also wrest state secrets from the minds governing foreign powers! Or answers to test questions from the teacher's subconscious! In either case, the usual definitions of the operation of the mind must be augmented.

Past Life Regression in General

By and large, the great proportion of people in past life regression find themselves as "common" individuals, members of the working class, farmers, small merchants and landowners. I tend to discount any regression which borders on the amazing, romantic or ones dealing with historic figures as fantasy material. Nonetheless, fantasy can reveal a great deal about any subject, so I will allow the "regression" to continue with that implicit understanding.

Technique: The past life regression technique you use will depend on the features of this type of regression you wish to emphasize.

For therapeutic or personal-interest work, you can allow a certain leeway that clinical or experimental work does not permit. Once the subject is hypnotized, you may use symbolic or allegorical suggestions, or direct "go back to . . ." statements, as you prefer. As with any hypnotic suggestion, successful regression depends on your tone of voice, and the conviction and sincerity you project. With that in mind, you can use literally any regression suggestions and still get good results. I like to add the suggestion that, "You will always be able to speak and understand English," as a precautionary measure, particularly for the foreign born.

The methods I find simple and effective follow:

Counting: With the subject already hypnotized, I state, "In a few moments, I will count backward from your present age to zero, and say the word 'transfer.' When I say 'transfer,' you will automatically transfer back into a past life, another place and time, another you, that has the greatest bearing on your present life. The mists of time and memory will clear, and you will be able to easily and naturally remember those important things." (If the subject is disposed toward unpleasant events, I might also include, "Going to a pleasant time only.") "Counting backwards now, as you move back in time. . . . 3 . . . 2 . . . 1 . . . 0 and transfer, all the way back to that important moment. Notice your surroundings . . ." Most subjects will take several minutes to fully enter the regression, and there may be long pauses between replies to your question. There is also a tendency for the subject to whisper, or he may evidence a disinclination to speak at all (aphasia). That's perfectly normal, and indicates that the subject is deeply involved with the regression.

The Corridor: For subjects whose imaginative powers are already in evidence, or those who are visual by nature, I use the leading idea of a long passageway or corridor, with doors on both sides. When the subject is hypnotized, I say, "You can walk down this corridor, noticing the doors on both sides. Each door is a past life you have lived. Each door holds the entire events of an individual life. As you continue down this corridor, one of these doorways will attract your attention. It will stand out for some reason. Tell me when you find that door. Now describe that door to me—material from which it is made, the color, etc. How do you feel about that door? Would you like to go through it?" (a way of obtaining unconscious permission). "In a moment, when you step through that door, you will step into an important event in that past life, something with special meaning to you. You'll be able to describe and discuss it in detail. Now, when you are ready, open that door, and step through. Notice your surroundings . . ."

This particular method of obtaining a past life regression would totally invalidate any experimental findings because it does lead so flagrantly. Therapeutically, it may stimulate some fantasy production, but it also produces results.

Experimental or clinical: You must be extremely careful about leading your subject when you are doing studies of past life regressions. However, some sort of end-point or focus is necessary to provide something for the subject to aim for. Therefore, to the hypnotized subject, I suggest, "In a few moments you will begin to go back in time, all the way back to something important happening. Your memory will become clear and vivid. You can go all the way back to the very beginning when that important something began to happen. Going all the way back, now, all the way until you are there. Tell me when you are there. Notice your surroundings. . . ."

I used an approach similar to this to bring one young man's first experience of fainting at the sight of blood to light. I initially thought that a possible childhood accident or some parental injunction had encouraged development of that rather ungainly habit. Given the above suggestions, he regressed to a courtyard scene, perhaps in Czarist Russia. He was looking up, frightened, as a large stone tower began to crumble. Unable to get out of the way in time, he felt the weight of the heavy rocks crashing down over most of his body. After some time, he dragged himself from the rubble and leaned up against a wall where, broken and covered in blood, he apparently passed into unconsciousness and died. Noticing the similarity of the "blood equals unconsciousness" in the regression and his present life, I suggested that the loss of blood suffered at that past time was hardly comparable to the drop or two he had been fainting at currently. Since the loss of a few drops of blood was not in any way detrimental, he could treat minor injuries in a different and more productive fashion. Follow-up indicates he has withstood the sight of blood without flinching since then.

It is past life regressions that happen like this one—without direct suggestion—that receive the most scientific interest. They can also be the most difficult to generate; the subject may reject as impossible any unusual or past life material himself, even before he shares it with you.

Information through questioning: When doing a past life regression, whether therapeutically or simply out of interest, I follow a format, one I've found conducive to bringing forth unusual and specific details. The questions I ask do not lead the subject, but instead encourage him to use the information at hand to supply an answer. They also help the subject move from the general to the specific in his memories, as follows:

1. Notice your surroundings. What place is this (inside or outside)?
2. Describe your surroundings, paying special attention to features that seem important.
3. Notice your position in these surroundings. Where are you? What position are you in (standing, sitting, etc.)?
4. Begin to notice yourself. Are you male or female?
5. How are you dressed?
6. Notice your hands. Describe them, and any jewelry you may wear.
7. What name would you like me to call you? (Rather than the demanding and hence threatening, "What is your name?")
8. How old are you?
9. What is the year?
10. Allow this memory to unfold: what is happening?
11. What happens next? What happens next?
12. Proceed to the time of your death. (If the subject is interested in pursuing this only. There may be great resistance here otherwise.)
13. The time is one minute before you died (notice past tense), and you are able to describe everything in detail.
14. How do you feel?
15. Describe the condition of your health.
16. How old are you?
17. Describe your location (others present?).
18. The time is one minute after you have died. Where is your body?
19. Where are you now? (For those so inclined, I may suggest that they are "hovering" just above the body, with

an incredible sense of freedom. This is a flagrant example of leading the subject. I excuse my behavior here by the expedient of saying that many subjects enjoy the thought of floating out beyond themselves, and find it a good vantage point to continue the regression.)

20. What happened next to your body?

21. Notice what arrangements were made to dispose of your body.

22. Describe what happened. (If there is a grave stone or marker, I'll ask them to read it. This not only provides a name and dates, but sometimes even an epitaph.)

Given the general nature of the preceding questions, the quality of the replies can be remarkable. Many will report particular interest in question six, expressing surprise at how different their hands are from what they expected. Many will be very amazed at being a person of the opposite sex.

An individual in past life regression may evidence the same strength of emotion found in abreactive work—tears, anger, panic, terror, guilt, etc. An occasional few have reactions that do not occur with traditional "present life" abreactive work:

One man described climbing a hillside in past life regression. Suddenly, in mid-sentence, he stopped talking—and breathing! I realized something had happened in the regression and quickly suggested he could view the scene from a safe distance. Apparently, he had been caught in an explosion and killed instantly. There had simply been no more to say. His body reflexes would have continued his breathing after a short time had elapsed; there was no danger of his death on my recliner. Other body systems did not stop—the breath holding was akin to "sudden surprise" rather than "instant death."[5] In such cases you may wish to aid the subject, as I did, into a recalled regression, but the body will return to normal on its own, regardless.

After awakening this man he recounted the abrupt experience of finding himself nowhere, "Like an intelligence, a knowing without thought. Very strange," he said, "and impossible to fully describe."

A young woman, who in her usual conscious state had no interest in jewelry of any sort, found herself as a male Persian artisan who specialized in turquoise. In regression, he was preoccupied with detailing certain decorative gems and rings he had made. When she was awakened from hypnosis, I removed my own set of silver and turquoise rings and bracelets and asked her to tell me about the stones. She immediately began a discourse on the quality of the gems, color, specific hardness, and why they were of little or no value! I kept my astonishment to myself: she was evidencing more knowledge about turquoise than I had.

The next day I was able to contact a recognized authority on Indian and Persian turquoise who confirmed each of her comments on color, hardness and mounting characteristics. The woman, unfortunately, was not pleased to hear this—she became fearful of the whole concept, especially about knowing things she had never studied—and refused to continue explorations any further!

Some Speculations on Age Regression

With the advent of the clinical hypnotist much of the prolonged work of analysis can be shortened or eliminated. When the purpose of traditional analysis is to bring lost memories, traumas, and hatreds to light, there can be nothing more expedient than hypnosis to reach those unconscious processes.

Sadly, many psychoanalysts have yet to discover how effective regression hypnosis can be. For whatever reason, there still seems to be the age-old prejudices floating around, waiting to drop into the professional's ear. Perhaps the hypnosis will be "too quick" for the subject to tolerate; maybe the client will worsen from knowing too much about himself; suppose he really can't tolerate the knowledge that he hated his mother; what if the hypnosis unleashes some hitherto confined anger that will no longer allow itself to be controlled? Wouldn't hypnotism then be responsible for turning a mass of crazed killers loose?

Somewhere along the way, it has been forgotten that the individual mind has its own series of controls, limits that it will not violate. No one kills after being hypnotized unless it was already an inclination they possessed before in one form or another. The act of age regression cannot bring forth any traits that the subject hasn't already learned to live with—but it can bring out very convincing and positive personal understandings for reaffirmation or correction. A subject can "learn" something in an age regression that will change his present.

Material which can be reusable as the result of regression doesn't necessarily have to be of great pathological importance, either. One study indicated that long (consciously) forgotten Latin conjugations could be made available to the current self, even if that information hadn't been used for several decades, and could be as useful as if it had just recently been learned. It is as though the mind can tune into past knowledge—of whatever sort—and bring that learning intact to the present. In other words, the freshness of a three-year-old's perception of springtime can be restored to the 40-year-old adult. The clarity of that positive experience might do a great deal for the individual who believes that nothing is new or worth living for.

Past life regression is another thing, however. The controversial aspects of whether or not reincarnation is an actuality or not make this type of regression ever suspect in our culture. A Buddhist may be perfectly at home discovering past life causes for present life difficulties . . . but anyone who espouses such a thing in our society is still considered a little "kooky." After all, just like personal "resurrection," reincarnation is an idea which lacks objective proof. Dates, names, places, and past life details which are uncovered in regression can be checked, verified and clearly established as fact, but that still does not convince the skeptic. There is no reason why it should. Past life regression can be done quite effectively without a belief in reincarnation. All it takes is a willingness to experience the *possibility*.

The individual in a past life regression may display traits in common with his present life existence. For example, he may currently have a profound interest in the American Civil War. In regression he may find himself on a Civil War battlefield, describing cannon shot and gunfire. Even this provides no genuine proof for or against the validity of reincarnation. He may have been interested in the Civil War because he once lived through it—or his interest in the Civil War may have prompted an age regression fantasy. A fear of cats may have "come" from being eaten by a lion in ancient Rome, or the fear of cats may promote an imagined reason for its own existence.

In the few cases where a person "learns" a new skill or trait *from* a regression lies the basis of most pro-reincarnation arguments. The woman I worked with who came out of regression with a "new" knowledge of turquoise is an example of this. But again, she was not willing to continue the experiments, so it may never be known if that actually was a past-life learning, a hoax, a coincidentally correct fantasy, an awakened childhood memory, or a case of telepathy.

To add complexity to an already overly complex issue, some hypnotists are discovering that regression experiments occasionally turn up individual past lives which overlap; that is, one life lived, for example, from 1735 to 1800, and another from 1773 to 1821. This unusual discrepancy leads to an "ah-hah!" of triumph for the skeptic: it couldn't possibly be "real" reincarnation then!

Dick Sutphen[6] postulates a reason for this, a parallel self of a vaster self simultaneously exploring life. Accordingly, it should be conceivable for a person in regression to "remember" this alternate lifetime and recall being born, for example, in 1950, as well as his "actual" birthdate, or to find himself living today in St. Louis and elsewhere, and be able to verify the actual details of that "other life" with known records.

The end to this is impossible to define. The further tangles in current reincarnation dogma which result throw monkeywrenches into the linear one-life-follows-another concept. Jane Roberts proposes a solution, of sorts, by expanding the reincarnation theories to include these also-living "counterparts."[7] Consequently—and I am greatly simplifying—the "soul" can consist of many selves which exist simultaneously, in all time periods. Yet, the skeptic will remain unconvinced; there is no hard and fast objective proof.

I am not encouraging or even suggesting a belief in reincarnation as a requisite for good hypnosis—or for anything for that matter. Personal beliefs should be kept personal. But I am allowing these conjectures and theories here because they have proven to be useful therapeutic tools. Since they do work, it is your obligation to your clients to understand, and be willing to use them, regardless of whether you believe it is "true" reincarnation or not.

To summarize, age regression can be a useful tool to the therapist, doctor or law enforcer. It is a system which can quickly recover consciously forgotten material. Regression may occur spontaneously, or it may be generated through hypnosis.

Techniques for assisting the client in producing a regression are varied. As with any hypnotic procedure, the hypnotist's confidence in the success of the outcome, and the subject's willingness to undergo the experience, are the vital factors. Subjects may react with great emotion during regression, or they may show few dramatic changes. It is the inner components of regression which make it work.

The next chapter demonstrates one way in which age regression is becoming useful.

NOTES TO CHAPTER SEVEN

1 This contention was the basis for an Oregon court battle a few years back. The hypnotists lost. In many states, testimony acquired through hypnosis is not admissible as evidence in court but, like the revelations of police-supported psychics, hypnotically derived information can be used as leads to track down suspected criminals.

2 *Scientology: The Now Religion*, by George Malko (Delta, 1970) provides interesting and fair insights into Scientology's purposes and techniques.

3 Morris Netherton, Ph.D., uses a Dianetics-style approach to his past life work, as explained in his *Past Lives Therapy* (William Morrow & Co., 1978).

4 Jeffery Iverson's *More Lives Than One?* (Warner Books, 1976) catalogs several regressions he personally researched. His objectivity is notable and resulted in a documentary for the BBC.

5 There are no documented cases of anyong dying in regression.

6 *Past Lives, Future Loves*, (Pocket Books, 1978). Sutphen is an Arizona hypnotist who has specialized in past life age

regression, having worked with thousands of people.

7 In both *Psychic Politics* (Prentice-Hall, 1976) and *The 'Unknown' Reality*, Volume 2, (Prentice-Hall, 1979), her presentation makes such an idea credible.

CHAPTER EIGHT

It's All in the Mind: Treating Illness with Hypnosis

Your beliefs about what is desirable and what is not, what is good and what is evil, cannot be divorced from the condition of your body . . .[1]

In recent years, there have been numerous studies to show that much, if not all, illness is rooted in the mind. This idea, of course, has been vigorously disputed in traditional medical circles. I do not propose in this chapter to argue with the proponents of germ theory; I merely wish to express an alternative idea which, having proven its value in treating disease, merits further investigation.

The study of the influence of the mind or emotions on physical health is "psychosomatics." "Psycho" comes from the ancient word meaning "mind"; "soma" from the word meaning "body." No one is surprised to hear talk of "tension headaches." Neither is the mention of "ulcer" and "repressed anger" in the same breath uncommon. What about ulcerative colitis, rheumatoid arthritis, asthma, hypertension, and cancer?

Hippocrates himself formulated a connection between illnesses and temperament . . . the long, lean, narrow-chested person was more inclined to tuberculosis than the rotund, robust type—who, on the other hand, was more likely to suffer a cerebral hemorrhage . . . diabetics are fond of the pleasures of the table, heart disease often occurs among the anxious, that peptic ulcer sufferers are frequently hard-driving go-getters.[2]

The science of psychosomatics is relatively new to Western medicine, still deeply immersed in Pasteur's theories that all illness is the outcome of a body being assailed by microbes. Yet, even Pasteur spoke of the importance and influence of the terrain—the body—with his dying words: "The microbe is nothing, the terrain is everything."[3]

Somewhere, perhaps, in the generations-long act of separating man from the natural elements in which this animal body once lived, a certain forgetfulness set in. Somehow, the intimate connection between the vital systems of body and mind became weakened in thought and theory, so much so that few remember how strong that bond had once been. The highly personal understanding of illness-as-feedback has been lost.

Our bodies are built of sterner stuff than we generally give them credit for. Certainly there are numerous illnesses, some catastrophic, and many that we perpetrate on ourselves by careless management of our bodies. Too many X-rays will do more damage than most of the lesions, broken bones and lodged foreign materials they are designed to locate.

Yet, a body given minimum supervision, nutrition, and care will last, in good health, for seventy or eighty years—or more. Think of the amount of alcohol that must be consumed before its effects becomes irreversible: gallons upon gallons, over the course of many years. People in underdeveloped countries may subsist on a nearly exclusive diet of rice for a lifetime. Bodies can tolerate extremes of temperature, from the tropics to the arctic, and can adjust to dramatic changes in altitude.

In this culture we have all but forgotten that we can survive the flu without patent medicines, endure a toothache without aspirin. We have lost the art of using our bodies as they were designed: an intimate, emotional feedback system.

That headache is not something visited upon the luckless by coincidence; it has a cause within the bodily system. It may arise from tension, from breathing polluted air, from eye-strain, from repressed anger, from constipation, from a tumor. But it is not *just* a headache, it is a symptom with significance and definite meaning. It is the body's way of making an important point—a "notice what is happening!" plea.

By ignoring or medicating away "minor" irritations like headaches and the flu, we ignore a vital message. By paying attention to the transitory pain, a lesson can be learned about what it means. If a headache comes from tension, the body's message is to avoid tension—utterly simple and unconfusing. But if that clue is disregarded long enough, the body has no chance to regenerate itself, no chance to recuperate. A tension headache, medicated, teaches nothing: its cause and purpose is neglected. The sufferer, because he has not heard the body's request for release from tension, continues his damaging practices. This may result in chronic bruxism (teeth grinding), muscle spasms in the shoulders and back, fatigue and, in extreme cases, emotional breakdown.

It takes effort to make a body sick, unremitting conscious

effort. The ulcer patient has spent a long time purposely ignoring the gas, stomach pain, irritation from specific foods, and the buried anger or tension that led up to his "sudden problem." Illness is not thrust upon a body; it is willingly accepted, encouraged, and courted.

Organic vs. Contagious

Here I must make a distinction between contagious illness (that spread by bacteria or other microscopic organisms) and organic illness (created by physical "malfunction"). In previous paragraphs I have written primarily of organic illness, and how by a lack of bodyfeedback awareness that disease is encountered. Contagious illness, however, has its roots in *both* emotional and physical mechanisms.

No two people exposed to the same set of bacterial invaders can be expected to acquire exactly the same results. There is a distinct correlation between general physical health and the acceptance of contagious disease. That is, if a person is "rundown," he or she will be more susceptible to whatever "bug" is making the rounds. To put it another way, by abusing your personal feedback system, you weaken it. So the young person who spends late evenings dancing, and falls asleep at work in the morning is a willing candidate for illness. Being tired all the time does not feel good. The body is trying to get a point across: sleep more. Again, by ignoring the obvious, a worse situation is invited. Contagion depends on more than proximity; it requires a special *willingness*.

Experimenters continue to uncover viruses and other organisms in connection with individual diseases, yet nearly all bodies carry the same "bugs." *Streptococci*, the one responsible for streptococcus infections ("strep throat"), can be routinely encountered on public telephones and during ordinary conversation—but most people will live out their entire lives without succumbing to that illness.

Research indicates that stress, change or emotional upset "weakens" or disarms the body—perhaps by misdirecting energies—enough so that ordinary, ever-present bacteria can multiply undisturbed, creating illness.

Not only that, specific mental attitudes, as in Type A behavior, can result in harmful or stressful energies being directed toward specific organs, without the intermediary of microbes. It's almost as if an organ is allowed to become "bad" as a symbol for the whole person.

Cancer of various sorts is generally associated with feelings of helplessness, hopelessness and chronic depression. These occur prior to the onset of the disease, too, not as a result of it. Yet several viruses have been linked to the disease. In cancer management the patient's attitudes are vitally important. Those who utterly give up succumb to the disease quickly. Those who continue to fight back often experience remission after remission.

Norman Cousins, author of *Anatomy of an Illness*, was diagnosed as having an ankylosing spine, a terminal, degenerative disease of the spinal column. Hospitalized, he was not an ideal patient—he refused to give more than one blood sample per day, insisting that the large amount taken at once could be shared by every hospital department that wanted any. Finally, fed up with hospital policy, and with his doctor's permission, he checked himself out and began a self-treatment program consisting of large doses of vitamin C and laughter. Certainly unconventional, but he survived, and the physical deterioration was arrested. Today he lectures on holistic medicine. He is a living testimonial to his beliefs.

That may be the key, *beliefs*. If the subject believes he must suffer illness, must deteriorate and eventually die in agonizing pain, nothing will help. No study has ever been able to connect the incidence of illness with standing in drafts, but many believe drafts *cause* colds. If the subject holds out hope or faith or confidence in his doctors, treatment or future, he may have a very good chance for a cure.

So, working with psychosomatic illnesses, the focus of assistance should be aimed at the subject's attitudes, whether viral infection is a component or not. The Type A person is slowed down, the anxious is calmed, the depressed cheered—not with artificial, outside enforcement, but with a concentrated *change* in his world view.

Conversion reactions: Guilt, fear and anger all play important roles in the production of a psychosomatic disease. When these feelings become too much to bear, the individual's unconscious mind may do what seems the most sensible: try to discharge the feeling into something that can be managed—physical illness.

In a conversion reaction, symptoms are generally expressed in parts of the body that are under conscious or voluntary control, such as the limbs. *La belle indifference*, beautiful indifference, may accompany the symptoms.

This beautiful indifference is a state of passive, almost tranquil peace, with no concern whatsoever for what may be happening to physical health. So the executive with an unexplained limp may outwardly appear to be perfectly content with his condition. Indeed he will be, because it has "solved" an enormous personal problem: "cured" his repressed feelings by generating them onto his body.

Needless to say, where there is peace and contentment there is no effort to seek better circumstances. That executive's limp—since the underlying need has not been erased—may progress to actual muscle degeneration and bone changes. But, remember, this is an act of self-preservation, regardless of how it may look to the observer. To this harried businessman, *nothing* is worse than dealing with those feelings, and many outcomes are preferable. He needs that symptom desperately.

Working with a subject who is operating under a conversion reaction may be complicated by *la belle indifference*. Treatment is frightening and threatening, so he may not show up for sessions or follow instructions. He must, however, eventually deal with the root cause, or there will be no improvement.

Emotional Factors in Psychosomatic Illness

There is no question that a healthy body or mind cannot survive without the other, though the influence of one upon the other has yet to be fully understood. Simple biofeedback experiments indicate that *each thought* produces a corresponding physical reaction, if only on a minor scale. Perhaps it is the constant repetition of specific thoughts which can lead to chronic health difficulties, so that the removal or absence of those thoughts allows the body to return to its natural state of health.

New studies show that the stress of personal change itself contributes a great deal to the onset of psychosomatic illness. *Psychosomatic Medicine*[4] includes a list compiled of commonly encountered life changes, giving each change quantitative "impact" units. It has been demonstrated that an accumulation of over 200 of these units in a year is associated with a high incidence of illness.

Stress of Adjusting to Change

Events	*Scale of Impact*
Death of spouse	100
Divorce	73
Marital separation	65
Jail term	63
Death of close family member	63
Personal injury or illness	53
Marriage	50
Fired at work	47
Marital reconciliation	45
Retirement	45
Change in health of family member	44
Gain of new family member	44
Pregnancy	40
Sex difficulties	39
Business readjustment	39
Change in financial state	38
Death of close friend	37
Change to different line of work	36
Change in number of arguments with spouse	35
Mortgage over $10,000	31
Foreclosure of mortgage or loan	30
Change in responsibility at work	29
Son or daughter leaving home	29
Trouble with inlaws	29
Outstanding personal achievement	28
Wife begins or stops work	26
Begin or end school	26

Change in living conditions	25
Revision of personal habits	24
Trouble with boss	23
Change in work hours or conditions	20
Change in schools	20
Change in recreation	19
Change in church activities	19
Change in social activities	18
Mortgage or loan less than $10,000	17
Change in sleeping habits	16
Change in number of family get-togethers	15
Change in eating habits	15
Vacation	13
Christmas	12
Minor violations of the law	11

So the stress of adjusting to change plays an important part in the generation of illness. Similarly, the action of the emotions themselves, brought into play by seven common factors, can account for the root of a psychosomatic disease:

1. *Organ language:* In our language, a reflection of inner realities, we often speak of outside conditions as if they were happening inside the body—"This job is a headache," is a prime example of organ language. Each such phrase or statement is a literal suggestion to the inner mind to associate the situation with the physical statement.

"I'm really burned up," "What a pain in the neck," "I can't stomach that," "It makes me tired," and so forth, are examples of statements that, with repetition, will create a corresponding physical outlet.

One 30-year-old man suffered from severe lower back

pain of unknown origin. He had tried adjustment, taps, spinal fusion and was considering having surgery to destroy the nerves in the afflicted area. He heard Raymond LaScola, M.D., a Los Angeles hypnotist, speaking one evening and during the question and answer period asked if anything could be done hypnotically to help him. LaScola listened for a few moments to the history of the complaint. He asked the man about his marriage. That was fine, he was assured. How about the man's job? That, replied the man, was "a pain in the ass!" LaScola spent all of one session suggesting that the man consider his job a "nuisance," not a pain. From that day, over five years ago at this writing, the man has suffered no recurrence of the pain.

A close relative of organ language is the "crying syndrome." This is the outward expression of tears or crying, concealed within a look-alike illness, such as a head cold. The resultant illness then allows the individual to legitimately express the feeling he could not otherwise bring out.

The act of crying involves not only the tear ducts, but includes the nasal mucus passages, the Eustachian tubes and frequently the entire breathing apparatus. Illnesses such as asthma, bronchitis, upper respiratory allergies, hay fever and so forth may be an expression of the crying syndrome. Dr. Franz Alexander of the Chicago Institute for Psychoanalysis says that most asthma patients report that it is difficult for them to cry. "Moreover," he says, "attacks of asthma have been repeatedly observed to terminate when the patient could give vent to his feeling by crying."[5]

A stoic 54-year-old executive went skiing with his 52-year-old wife. The woman slipped and broke a leg on the slopes, so the trip was cut short. The executive returned to work, even though his wife suffered complications and had to be hospitalized. On the first day of her hospitalization, he developed a dramatic headcold. His sneezing and tearing eyes ran through several boxes of tissue each day for the week of his wife's hospital stay. The day his wife was discharged, his headcold disappeared. Unable to consciously accept his expression of natural sorrow over his wife's condition, his body—and unconscious mind—did so for him, through the crying syndrome.

2. *Identification:* Children grow by copying and identifying with their parents. The child will develop similar mannerisms and habits as the parents, and may also acquire parental complaints. For example, a woman gives her nine-year-old son a vitamin pill to swallow. She also hands him a large glass of water and says, "Be careful, now, that your throat doesn't close up. Mine always closes up. If it does, just take a big sip of water." Needless to say, given this type of encouragement, the boy chokes on the pill and requires huge gulps of water to get it down. The woman insists that it "runs in the family." Her mother, too, couldn't take oral medication easily.

A 48-year-old man suffers the symptoms of a heart attack on the anniversary of his father's death from a heart attack. He may be experiencing the "anniversary syndrome," an identification with the parent with concurrent physical manifestations. A woman undergoes an asthma-like attack each year on the anniversary of her divorce. It is the timing, the date, which becomes significant in this syndrome, as well as the identification with someone else.

Identification doesn't necessarily have to be with one's parents. The subject can sense an identification with any figure of authority or admiration. A beloved uncle or favorite teacher may be the object of the identification. The results are the same, nevertheless.

3. *Conflict:* This may be one of the most powerful causes of psychosomatic difficulties. Conflict appears when there

is a need or wish to do something, but restrictions of society or conscience prevent it.

Sexual conflicts abound among those raised in childhood with one set of beliefs, then exposed in adolescence or adulthood to other principles. Our society is also patently aggression and hostility repressed. Repressing a need to be aggressive may result in a conflict problem, which in turn expresses itself somatically. The solution to this may be too simple to really appreciate: express the aggression. But . . .

> Suppose I feel like killing my boss, then, or putting poison in my husband's tea; or worse, hanging my five children on the clothesline instead of the towels? Are you saying that I should merely follow through? . . . The fact is that before being "assailed" by what may seem to be such terrifying unnatural ideas, you have already blocked off an endless variety of far less drastic ones, any of which you could have expressed quite safely and naturally in daily life.[6]

The individual suffering a conflict problem divides his beliefs into "acceptable" and "unacceptable" categories. He teaches himself to ignore the unacceptable ones, hiding them from himself deep in the unconscious. The conscious mind may be fooled, but the body is not, and does not forget.

If the unacceptable thought is too horrifying, the individual may develop the conversion reaction, turning that somatic component into a symbolic expression of the aggressive feeling. For example, a man who wishes to strangle his boss may awaken with tension or numbness in his hands and arms. One surgeon developed a marked hand tremor while in military service. Under hypnosis he spoke of a desire to get his commanding officer "on the table." Using an abreactive technique in conjunction with the creation of that possibility in his mind, he mentally and gleefully "operated" on the officer. When the session was concluded, his tremor was gone. The conflict was resolved by acting it out.

4. *Motivation:* It may be a surprise to discover that a person's illness can actually serve a constructive purpose in his life. It may give the individual something to talk about, make them "special," prevent them from doing whatever they don't wish to, etc. The mind is goal directed; the problem may fill a need perfectly.

On the evening her husband got box seats to a World Series baseball game, a woman developed an intense headache. Nauseated and pale, she moaned pitifully until the husband agreed to stay home. By the time the game was over, the headache was gone. That was to be expected, since the reason for the pain had been served: to keep her husband home.

5. *Masochism:* Self-punishment can be a powerful motivator in its own way. The woman student mentioned in the previous chapter who had the allergy to cats may have been punishing herself for prior behavior.

To the observer, the severity of the punishment exacted for past "crimes" may be way out of line, often excessive and compulsive. It is as if the unconscious mind replays the "crime" *as it was* and holds that up for constant scrutiny; all the intervening masochistic compensations are ignored.

One young woman developed the inability to swallow any solid foods. Unexpectedly, she gained rather than lost weight, concentrating her meals around milk shakes, mashed potatoes and the like. She could not tolerate any meat products. Age regression produced an adolescent memory fraught with personal conflicts: she had performed fellatio on a popular boy, hoping to get special attention from him. When that attention was not forthcoming, she realized the gruesomeness of her "crime," and sought to punish herself for her actions. Not only could she no longer take that "meat" in her mouth—or any kind of meat—but she gained enough weight to make herself unattractive. Yet, somewhere in her unconscious, the evil deed was not paid for: she could have continued to develop new symptoms because of just one sexual encounter.

6. *Past experience:* Each experience teaches. If Tommy learns that having a legitimate stomach ache gets him out of school for a day, he may discover that he can acquire a stomach ache anytime he wants one. When Tommy grows up, he may not consciously remember how or when he made the decision to have stomach aches to get out of undesirable situations. His inner mind will remember, however, and use that highly workable system whenever he needs it.

You might also expect to find a past experience at the root of beneficial behaviors. Tommy learned, too, that he could get special attention from Mom when he brought home a good report card. As an adult, Tommy works to his capacity and does a good job. Where most of the other factors in psychosomatic illness may prove ultimately detrimental, past experience always includes some positive learnings.

7. *Effects of Suggestion:* We often hear "power of suggestion" to explain any coerced behavior, and that is not quite accurate, technically speaking. "Suggestion" itself has no more innate power than the perceiver lends it. Authority figures wield more "suggestive power" than their followers, but only because that power is given them by their "inferiors." Suggestion of various sorts can have lifelong effects.

The boy with the difficulty swallowing pills was a subject of such suggestion—the subtle, pervasive influence of Mother, who "could do no wrong." Whenever an authority is acknowledged, that power-figure will exert some influence on his or her subjects. The boss says, "Work hard—you may get a raise," and his suggestion is heeded. There is no promise of increased funds, no real statement of any intent, just a vague encouragement.

In a similar manner, when suggestion is coupled with a physical enforcement, such as a slap or spanking, that suggestion takes on added significance. The father who spanks his child while saying "You're no good," is instilling a suggestion. One famous case occurred in such a way: A woman slapped her rebellious pre-school daughter saying, "Don't you ever say 'No' again!" The little girl learned from that one instance never to say no—to anyone or anything. As an adult, she continually found herself in unsavory sexual situations because of it, did unpaid overtime work, and generally had a miserable time. To counter this, she was instructed to say "no" to the hypnotist. Either way, she was headed for a resolution of her difficulty: if she said "no," or refused to say it—thereby saying "no"—she found that she didn't have to follow that suggestion any longer.

Any of these seven emotional components can operate alone or in conjunction with another, but at least one of them will be at the root of any psychosomatic problem.

Psychosomatic Ills

Of the many diseases now considered psychosomatic in origin, the following is a listing of the most common, with possible generating factors. This is provided so that you can graphically note possible emotional components of the particular illness, and as a guideline to working with clients having these complaints. Of course, it is not a final listing, and should be viewed as the opening wedge rather than as an inflexible rule applicable in each case.

Disease	*Factor*
asthma, bronchitis	crying syndrome
hypertension	repressed anger
cancers	hopelessness, depression
dermatitis, psoriasis	anxiety, guilt
ulcerative colitis	repressed rage
vaginismus	sexual guilt
rheumatoid arthritis	resentment, anger
backache	repressed attack desires
tics	anxiety
constipation	fear of loss
tinnitus	anxiety
anorexia nervosa	sexual anxiety
migraine	unexpressed frustration
pneumonia, flu	crying syndrome
contact dermatitis	passivity, deprivation
osteoarthritis	fear of change

It is also interesting to note that diseases which remain "hidden" within the body, such as ulcers or tumors, include a further implication that the psychological component is being ignored or kept unconscious. Psychosomatic ills that appear on the body surface or in muscle groups seem to be symptoms of problems which are working themselves out, or coming to completion.

Difficulties in Treating Psychosomatic Ills

The primary difficulty in working with an individual with a suspected psychosomatic complaint is the amazing flexibility of the unconscious mind. It is just short of ridiculous to assume you or I can fully understand and appreciate another person's true motives and actions, especially when that individual doesn't consciously know them himself. In the past history of hypnosis, direct suggestion has often been used to eradicate unwanted behaviors, without a thorough understanding of the underlying unconscious need for that action. It is the inner mind's innate flexibility which allows it to continue the unwanted behavior in another guise, as long as that *need* exists.

To the ex-smoker who suddenly finds he cannot stop eating, that unconscious need is a reality played out in his everyday life. He may feel as though he has no choice in the matter—that he is compelled to perform that action by some inner force, greater than the self he knows. Certainly the unconscious mind can accept a suggestion to eliminate any given habit—and will replace those it considers necessary with another habit, often of a less desirable nature.

Consequently, when working with a psychosomatic illness, you must allow the unconscious the opportunity to express the underlying cause of the problem, not simply whisk it away through forceful suggestion. Hypnotism received a considerable portion of its bad name from such "symptom transference," caused by careless management of the subject.

Imagination: There are those individuals whose overall physical health is good, but who claim to suffer from various diseases. These "hypochondriacs" live in just as much fear of their "illness" as someone who actually suffers the given disease. I do not intend to subtract from the imaginary illness's influence on the sufferer. Even an "imaginary" fear of heart failure can produce intense anxiety in the individual—each unusual heartbeat becomes a warning that disaster is near. There are cancerophobias as well, a fear of cancer so powerful that the person may plan his will and bid farewell to his earthly goods, yet remain in perfect health.

Generally, the individual with an imaginary complaint cannot be reassured to the contrary by a medical diagnosis. He is completely convinced of his near-mortality. There seems to be an intense anxiety at the root of this type of reaction. It is this state of anxious concern—over other life situations—which produces the concentration on illness. Understandably, the focus on life-threatening illness overshadows other personal problems so that it makes them less fearsome.

In its own way, imaginary illness is similar to a conversion reaction, where fears of one sort are transferred onto another medium. In this imaginary form, that medium is not the body, but the person's *emotional contact* with his body. He wishes to be ill in order to direct his attention away from what makes him most anxious. The primary difference is the fact that no organic disease actually exists. The hypochondriac may simply be looking for some good, loving care—of which he can never get enough.

In working with this client, and all sufferers of psychosomatic illness, extreme care must be taken to honor their belief in disease—it is the only protective wall they have against more frightening "monsters." Treating a psychosomatic illness, then, requires a specialized approach.

Treating the Psychosomatic Illness

Because psychosomatic diseases are generated out of a basic unconscious need, the process of helping the subject to understand and eliminate that need is the foundation of any treatment. Reaching the point where the client is willing to open to you the secrets he has kept hidden even from himself will require rapport, your good timing, a nonjudgmental attitude and a sense of extreme honesty, as well as hypnotic technique.

Rapport and good timing: The client never wanted to admit, particularly to himself, that he believed he couldn't live in an adult world. But that almost-hidden, nagging doubt plagued him for years. At age 28, while sipping the second cup of coffee he had ever had, he said, "Coffee always meant adulthood to me . . . I can understand why I wouldn't drink it before." We shared a third cup before the session officially began.

Rapport and timing are crucial but often neglected parts of hypnosis. Some people adjust to new ideas about themselves quickly. Others need weeks or even months to accept a new self-image. You simply cannot rush the client's unconscious mind, particularly after that inner mind has spent years developing one picture, one illness, for what it considers a very worthwhile purpose. It requires time to develop new world views.

Unconscious consent must precede any work. Again, the conscious mind does not necessarily have to participate in the process of giving approval—although that shouldn't be discouraged. Be aware of the unconscious movements and nods that indicate agreement or disagreement with your proposals . . . and if a negative response occurs, it is pointless to continue: the client may cooperate with your instructions, but the inner learning will not be complete. Each step should be built on the previous one.

Attitude and honesty: Because so many psychosomatic illnesses begin with feelings of guilt or fear, the client may be hesitant to express his thoughts. If your attitude is one of, "What, you, afraid of little teeny birdies? That's the stupidest thing I ever heard!" it will probably be the last dealing you have with that subject.

Similarly, if you reach a point where you are stumped by what has been happening, you might as well admit it to the subject. He has probably sensed it already anyway and will appreciate your straightforwardness. But this is not to suggest that you should stop your efforts at that point. On the contrary, by admitting your confusion, you open your own inner doors to alternative solutions. The subject may even offer a few ideas, direct from his own unconscious mind. In the same vein, if you believe the subject is making no progress, admit it—perhaps you'll find out why.

Hypnotic technique: It is in working with psychosomatic complaints that you'll discover how skilled you really are, as far as technique goes. There is no one approach that works with everyone, no guaranteed system. You will be using everything you know, from age regression through metaphors and reframing, watching for those unconscious responses that let you know you are following the right trail.

Very generally, I devote several sessions to developing rapport with the client, making him comfortable and relaxed in my surroundings. Hypnotically, we spend time with anchoring responses of self-assurance and well-being—which I invariably use later. I make a point of eliciting a series of hypnotic phenomena to help the subject understand that permanent, useful change can occur—almost an analogy of what we expect to happen with his psychosomatic complaint.

If the subject is willing, I probably will opt for age regression, allowing him to re-experience that event or series of events which led into his disease. As with any age regression, I would most likely ask him to repeat the events over and over until the emotional value is exhausted—and perhaps suggests some insight. For the subject who is aware of how he would like to express his feelings—like the surgeon mentioned earlier—it might be useful to have him act out that desire. Otherwise, I would proceed into a reframing approach, having the subject "talk" to the part responsible for the illness, discover its intention, and deal with it in a positive fashion.

After distinct improvement is seen, the subject is discharged. If the improvement is not "complete," further work may be necessary. I do a follow-up on a monthly basis for about six months, having the subject return for more hypnosis if there is any relapse or symptom transference.

Notes to Chapter Eight

1 *Nature of Personal Reality,* Jane Roberts (Prentice-Hall, 1974), page 141.

2 *Psychosomatics, How Your Emotions Can Damage Your Health,* Howard R. and Martin E. Lewis (Pinnacle Books, 1975), page 68.

3 *Can You Wait Till Friday?*, Ken Olson, Ph.D., (Fawcett Crest Books, 1975), page 250.

4 *Psychosomatic Medicine, Its Clinical Applications* (Harper and Row, 1977) Wittkower and Warnes, page 7, and designed

by Louis Linn, M.D. of Mt. Sinai Hospital, New York. Taken from an article in the New York Times by T. J. Holmes, dated June 10, 1973.

5 *Psychosomatics*, page 235.

6 *Nature of Personal Reality*, page 144.

CHAPTER NINE

Pain and Healing

Everyone becomes ill, harbors a disease, or breaks a bone at some time in his life. An organic complaint is one which bears some tissue change or damage . . . it is an actual, experienced alteration of the body structure, whatever its cause.

When a body is ill, and it is a time of crisis, the healing mechanisms are set in motion. When diseased, a body is not so much succumbing to circumstances as rallying its considerable forces for battle; it is a time of focusing energies on the vital physical mechanisms to counteract invading bacterial forces or repair functional damages.

When organic disease occurs, the body is removed from its "normal" patterns. It is the process of helping the body return to its natural state of good health that we call a "cure" or "healing."

Curing and healing can come about through numerous means: drugs, acupuncture, hypnosis, surgery, faith-healing, "psychic healing," even through quackery. But it is the body of the one afflicted that must do the healing; no procedure will keep someone healthy who desires illness. Neither doctor nor hypnotist promote cures or health where it is not wanted. Where strong motivation for health exists, there is excellent groundwork for healing. The power of the "will to live" has been shown thousands of times to triumph over phenomenal odds.

I do not wish to imply that a desire for health alone will produce it, particularly where an individual is already under medical guidance. If a subject is consulting a physician, he should continue to do so. The mode of treatment is extremely important. A portion of the client's belief system can assist in generating healthful thoughts. Your work can be aimed at assisting the client's faith in the medical treatment to produce desired results.

We're dealing in this chapter with both minor discomfort illnesses, such as broken bones, and catastrophic diseases like cancer. I'll begin where the illness generally does: with pain.

Pain

Pain is a subjective experience, frequently accompanying tissue damage, and associated with a variety of physical states having little in common except for the quality of bodily discomfort.

Like pleasure, pain was once thought to be purely mental in nature, having no physical correlative. As late as the 1950's, it was scientifically believed that newborn babies felt nothing. In 1970, in a science course, I watched the instructor jab a needle into a laboratory frog's brain; he insisted it couldn't feel anything as it wriggled in response to his jerks of the pin. I often wondered if that instructor would respond the same "painless" way to an instrument in his brain . . . if that superficial attitude could change once *his* subjective reality was invaded.

The highly personal interpretation of pain makes it difficult to work with in a clinical setting. How much does an illness *really* hurt? In an attempt to standardize pain research, a device called the dolorimeter[1] was developed. In terms of *dols*, the severity of any given pain was ascertained by application of controlled heat to a small area of skin surface. Accordingly, a set of "normal" pain levels was established, including:

toothache	2 dols
migraine	5
average male tolerance	6
burns	7–8
childbirth	10½
passing kidney stone	10½

The upper limit to the dolorimeter was set, by experimentation, at 21 dols[2]. However, after about 11 dols, most individuals gratefully pass into unconsciousness.

Even with the application of the dolorimeter, no truly standardized understanding of pain has been universally accepted. I have sufferered, for example, toothaches that were more severe than any sensations I experienced in an unsupervised, unanesthesized childbirth. Two clients of mine discussed their migraine headaches between appointments—"My migraine is much worse than anyone else's: I have to lie down for a half day!", "But mine is even worse than that . . . I throw up and wish I was dead!" Personal interpretation, tolerance, and nature of the disease involved all color the picture of pain as a modern condition.

Types of Pains

Analysis of pain begins with its most objective feature: its relationship to organic damage. Tissue damage falls into two main categories:

Injury: pain from injury includes that experienced as a result of cuts, bruises, tears, scrapes, burns and broken bones.

Illness: pain associated with illness includes that occurring with arthritis, cancer, pleurisy, ulceration, aneurism and angina.

Pain can also happen in a third and separate category, that caused entirely by the mind, without any organic basis. In this group are included stress-related pains where no organic damage has taken place. Factors which produce pain in this manner are: schizophrenia, phobias, muscle tension, childbirth and emotional upset.

The amount of pain felt in injuries tends to vary with the subject's emotional attitude and awareness of his physical condition. That is, the car accident victim may not fully realize he has been injured until he sees blood, or a bystander asks, "Does it hurt?"

With illness, focus is already directed at the organic damage, so pain of some sort may be expected and consequently appears. Attitude again plays a part, as well as hope for recovery.

Very generally speaking, the amount of pain felt in any circumstance will vary with the intensity of the experience, but it is not necessarily proportional. When tissue damage is severe enough, nerves which transmit sensory or pain impulses may be destroyed so that nothing registers correctly. A fatal burn may be experienced as entirely painless, while stepping on a tack—a very minor injury—can be accompanied by intense pain.

The individual's state of mind, physical health and tolerance to pain also play a part in the experience of pain. Included here would be the action of any physically or emotionally altering condition, such as drug or alcohol consumption, anger, sexual excitement, or a state of shock.

Experimental work with dental patients indicates that

the use of simple distraction can eliminate pain. Subjects had teeth filled, extractions performed and a few root canals excavated while listening to "white noise"[3] through earphones. The hissing sound of the white noise apparently provided a distracting element so that less pain was felt—or more pain was tolerated.

But pain is not necessarily bad. Obviously, it is the body's warning system, activating important defense mechanisms. Touching a hot stove produces an immediate, self-protective physical reaction. For this reason, pains of unknown origin should not be arbitrarily altered through hypnosis. That achy feeling, for example, in the right lower abdomen could be the result of too many pizzas, or it could be appendicitis . . . but it is an indicator that warns of an internal problem. As such, it should be respected.

Furthermore, having pain may be accompanied by "secondary gain," that good reason for having a specific pain continue. As with motivations for maintaining an illness, as described in the last chapter, having pain may make good conversation, keep the sufferer from performing unwanted activities, secure attention and so forth. If that type of pain is eliminated without consideration for the secondary gain, the subject may need to develop a more severe symptom.

Subjective analysis of pain: Much of the work done with hypnosis relies on the subject's analysis of his condition on a purely unconscious level. In determining what is happening to the client who is experiencing pain, the most workable system is to have him describe his feelings. The terms the client uses can indicate the pain's subjective severity. This must still be tempered by personal variations: a chronic complainer may find a hangnail excruciating.

Descriptive terminology tends to proceed from the tolerable to the extreme, as follows:

dull pain
aching
niggling
cramping
throbbing
choking
grinding
burning
twisting
tearing
stabbing
excruciating
lacerating
lightning
killing

But this is relative within the individual and not to be compared between several sufferers: his "throbbing pain" may be experienced as more severe than your "lightning" pain. By your client's description, you may assume that if he experiences a "stabbing" pain, it's probably worse than one he would describe as "dull" or "aching."

I do realize this is hardly a scientific method of comprehending the client's condition—but it is as specific as we can get without establishing arbitrary standards. It is something on the order of analyzing colors. We all agree that red is red, but how subtle is the difference between orange-red and red-orange?

One man, a printer, described an accident of having molten lead poured over the fingers of one hand. "I ran around the room twice before I knew what happened," he said. "It was like the feeling you get when you hammer a thumb—a kind of throbbing, achy feeling." With that description, you would be able to develop a fairly clear picture of the feelings involved.

Interestingly, having the subject locate and describe his pain will tend to diminish it. It is almost as if the act of focusing on the pain with the intention of defining it can contain it, or make it more objectively bearable.

The elimination of pain can act as a strong booster for the subject toward the goal of healing. Certainly, when the distracting element of pain is removed, the subject can more confidently focus on health; a sense of hopefullness prevails. The control or alteration of pain additionally produces a sense of self-determination and independence, particularly if the subject has been made a useful part of his own treatment rather than an observer of the process.

Treating Pain

Beyond the traditional modalities of pain control—medication—lies a vast and largely untapped field. Some experimenters are working with biofeedback, psychotherapy, and acupuncture, and are coming up with consistent results. Hypnotism has been used as a pain control device since antiquity.

Children learn a response to pain by how much attention and reward their injuries receive. When the parents supply Junior with extra attention after he has fallen, or has been sick, the child learns that illness and injury are preferred states. He may become "accident prone" in order to attract special notice, or may eventually become a hypochondriac. On the other hand, if health receives parental attention, and injury or illness is largely and reasonably downplayed, the child comes to understand which is the desirable condition. This positive reinforcement of the preferred state can only enforce it.

Having a consistent or unremitting pain alters the suffering individual in subtle ways. He may begin to believe his body has turned against him; he loses faith in the future; he may become depressed, irritable, hopeless or suicidal. Generally speaking, people living in the United States have a lower overall tolerance to painful conditions than Europeans do, and tend to equate pain with failure. In other countries, pain is seen and experienced as simply another facet of life, bearable and, to some degree, expected. Unfortunately, because of the American reliance on sources outside the individual, personal action in pain control is ignored. Using hypnosis for this problem, then, must emphasize the subject's own power to alter his condition—a part of the entire self-generated process of healing.

There are several approaches to pain control which can be used hypnotically:

Distraction: As with white noise, the subject's concentration is placed on something other than his physical discomfort. The pain remains intact, but is superseded by another topic. This can be accomplished as simply as asking the subject to describe his family, home, job or favorite hobby. While his focus is on that subject, he will be less aware of his pain.

In the same fashion, focus can be directed toward a portion of the subject's condition or other treatment. "Tell me if you feel anything in that left knee," will distract from everything but the left knee. I recall, as a child, going to visit the doctor for inoculations. Having received shots before, I was afraid of the pain the needle would cause, and was prepared to let the entire office know. But the doctor—a very serious, austere man—said he would put something on the spot to keep it from hurting. He produced a cotton ball which he saturated with a pungent liquid.

"There," he said, "now you won't feel a thing when I give you your shot. You can even watch if you like."

Sure enough, the vaccination was painless. After that I always asked for the medicine to "make it not hurt." Years later, I was to smell that pungent aroma again . . . it was nothing more exotic than isopropyl alcohol and not an anesthetic. By paying such good attention to the doctor's sincere statements—and having excellent motivation—I avoided the discomfort from the inoculation.

Dave Elman, mentioned in Chapter One, suggests a three-step approach using hypnosis:

1. ask the subject to concentrate on his favorite sport.
2. have the subject ascertain that he is really experiencing concentrated participation in that sport.
3. tell the subject that as long as he focuses on that activity, nothing will bother or disturb him.

When the subject cooperates, this works beautifully.

Incidentally, when using a distraction approach, as little attention should be focused on the word "pain" as possible. "Discomfort" is preferable in all situations, and beyond that, avoid references to any sensations other than pleasant and relaxing ones.

Alteration: Because the experience of pain is so nebulous, indirect hypnotic suggestion can be used to change pain from one sensation into another. If the subject's unconscious is in agreement, you may be able to suggest that a generalized pain be localized. For example, pain in the entire arm can be localized to the little finger of the hand. In some situations, the subject may accept an alteration of the pain into another sensation such as heaviness or numbness.

Part of the success of this approach is securing the unconscious mind's cooperation and willingness to have a sensation other than pain. Again, where pain does exist, so does good motivation, so your approach should include the expectancy of pain control.

Repetition: This is particularly effective in sudden or emergency situations, where pain is the direct result of an identifiable accident. The initiating incident is then repeated or mentally replayed several times, until a diminishing of the pain occurs.

Basically, the act of repeating the painful event creates a kind of physical catharsis. The accident becomes less drastic with each review, and subsequently loses its emotional impact.

Don't worry about hypnotizing the subject in an accident situation—the mind takes its own automatic steps to produce "separation" from the happening. With very mild encouragement, most accident sufferers slip easily into hypnosis and respond accordingly—even a suggestion as light as "Would you like that pain to go away?" can produce profound hypnosis. Once again, the motivation is good, and results will follow.

Elimination: The elimination of pain entirely can ease the effects of any unnecessarily painful occurrence, such as surgery or the setting of broken bones. However, elimination should be used with one stipulation, that should infection or secondary injury occur at any time, the pain will return. This prevents the person from overextending himself beyond his physical capacity by acting as a reminder of his current limits.

One young woman suffered muscular damage to one shoulder during a car accident. She was taught to eliminate that pain as long as she kept the shoulder relatively immobile as an aid to healing. However, one day she apparently overtaxed the shoulder at work and triggered a sudden onset of pain . . . a warning she took graciously by going home to rest.

This type of hypnotic anesthesia can be produced by the same means as glove anesthesia (discussed in Chapter

Five). Past experiences with numbness, such as through novocain or chilling, are invoked hypnotically, then transferred to the appropriate spot. For example, one man preparing for dental surgery was instructed to allow his hand to tingle and become numb. When he was certain the hand was without feeling, he was told to place it on his jaw, paying particular attention to how deeply the numbness went into his teeth, jaw and tongue. When the hand was removed, the mouth was left numb; it would be touched again after surgery to transfer the numbness back into the hand.

Visualization: This is the technique that has received the greatest media publicity for its usage in the treatment of various malignancies. Without doubt, it can be most effective when used with the subject's personal symbolism. This is best illustrated by example:

The pain is located within the body by visualizing a large human form diagrammed on a screen, with pain or injury seen as dark or hot spots or however the subject prefers. The spots are then the primary focus, with hypnotic instruction given to lighten or cool—even eliminate—the pain areas.

Variations on this have the "good army" (white blood cells) fighting the "bad army" (cancerous cells); the powerful "dragon" (white cells) eating the "food" (cancerous materials); and so forth. With this alteration, the focus is more on healing than on pain control and the treatment spans a longer period of time. Results have been very promising using this technique, demonstrating that the mind can control, or at least bring to remission, one of modern mankind's most dreaded illnesses.

Emphasis when using visualization is on the subject's own mental pictures, with as little outside suggestion as possible. In this way, the subject begins taking responsibility for his pain control early in the program, and is more easily encouraged to continue than he would be otherwise.

HEALING WITH HYPNOSIS

Healing is an entirely natural process which occurs spontaneously. Bodies are designed to heal themselves from the various scrapes, cuts, wounds and illnesses which nature has made a part of this life.

There are factors which may affect the individual healing process, factors with origins found in the essence of self-responsibility. No one can force another to heal, any more than one can produce illness in someone else.

Individual healing is colored by mental attitudes. It is not uncommon for the sick person to experience "regression" to earlier types of behavior: they become childish in demands and reasoning, refusing responsibility for their own health. Accompanying regression may be passivity, dependence on medical personnel, and the elusive secondary gain. There is a further lack of acceptance of the role the person can play in his own healing. In a manner of speaking, the fact that a hypnotist is called to work on such a case further reinforces the aspects of the subject's lack of control over his situation.

Initial hypnotic suggestions should be aimed at encouraging the subject's active participation in his healing—supporting his healthful advice and his positive concepts of health. Continued positive reinforcement must be a portion of this approach, with the subject's passivity and so forth similarly discouraged.

As a general and brief guide, some suggestions that may be used with specific complaints are included:

Broken bones: After the bones have been set and the

pain attended to, the physical process of healing becomes paramount. When a broken bone becomes an interference in job performance or other activities, such as for a professional athlete, suggestion can be used to speed the healing.

The subject is first shown pictures or diagrams of the affected bones in normal condition. Hypnotic suggestion is directed toward visualizing bones growing together rapidly, stronger than before. Indirect suggestions to the unconscious mind can be used to encourage the production of necessary tissues for healing in the afflicted area. If any pain occurs after the injured portion is in a cast, it should be checked by the attending physician immediately.

Surgery: Given the varieties of surgeries in use today, hypnosis can be used both as an anesthetic and to assist healing.

Medical personnel may be advised that the "unconscious" subject will hear and retain everything under discussion during his surgery—both when he is hypnotized and when he is under chemical anesthetic. The inner mind operates constantly, recording and storing information whether the conscious mind participates or not. Surgery conversation should be kept to a constructive minimum. One case of a woman's persistent abdominal pain following an appendectomy revealed that the attending surgeon had made some comment to the effect that she would "just have to live with it," meaning the surgery scar. Her inner mind, under general anesthesia, interpreted that to mean "the pain" of the operation. Age regression uncovered the cause, and insightful suggestions relieved the problem entirely.

As an anesthetic, hypnosis is indicated where the subject faces danger in the use of traditional anesthesia; where there is heart disease or other complications, or where the person's wakeful participation in the surgery is called for.

Glove anesthesia is again the preferred approach, transfering the numbness from the hand to the part to be operated on. Be sure to include a thorough description of the surgical procedure to be used, so that the subject can understand what is happening to his body.

Post-operatively, hypnosis can be used to alter or eliminate unnecessary pain, particularly that without physical origins, but an agreement should be made with the subject's unconscious mind that if infection or other difficulties arise, the pain will instantly return as a warning device.

Similarly, suggestions can be given to speed the post-operative healing process, and to describe the skill of the surgeon and the body's innate capacity to return itself quickly to good health.

Burns: Whether it is because fire was discovered late in man's evolution or for some other reason, bodies adapt worse to burns than to other injuries. There is a rapid loss of fluid and consequent dehydration; there may be extreme pain which is hard to relieve because of the medical complications.

Hypnotic suggestion should be geared toward retention of moisture, rapid tissue growth and distraction from the pain. It is also possible to suggest that pain diminish in proportion to the healing as an indicator of progress.

Since the danger of infection is so high, suggestions should be included which support the body's ability to resist invading microbes. Here, visualization techniques may be used advantageously.

Finally, don't ignore the supportive elements of the client's family and friends. Their loving reinforcement of self-help behavior and discouragement of dependencies can only aid the healing. In most cases, too, the organic difficulty can be creatively viewed as a "challenge" rather than a personal burden. That will lessen the intensity of the pain and make healing more of an adventure than an endless battle.

NOTES TO CHAPTER NINE

1 Dolorimeter: the name is derived from the Latin *dolor* meaning "pain," the same root as "Dolores" (the painful one), and dolorous (unpleasant).

2 According to Taber's *Cyclopedic Medical Dictionary*.

3 White noise is an electrically produced sound, reminiscent of the sound of ocean waves lapping at the shore. Listening to white noise seems to produce a very relaxed and receptive frame of mind.

CHAPTER TEN

Further Practical Applications of Hypnosis

Having shared some ideas on the use of hypnosis in the treatment of illness, pain and healing, it's time to advance the "practical" hypnotic viewpoint, the uses to which hypnotism is put on a daily basis.

There is no vaster field of hypnotic practice right now than habit control. There is practically no one who doesn't have some kind of annoying or persistent habit he'd like to be rid of—from smoking, to nail biting, to being overweight, to lack of concentration. Habit patterns respond to hypnotic suggestion, and it is in this area that most hypnotic practitioners make their living. This is not to say that habit control is a simple or easy procedure: ask anyone who has tried to lose thirty pounds! Nothing is quite so frustrating.

Let me reiterate here that a habit is initiated because the mind feels a strong need for it. The habit is begun out of need, repeated through conditioned response, and is difficult to shed because of the Law of Reversed Effect: where doubt is involved, the harder one tries, the less one is able to do. The unhappy habituated person keeps trying, and failing.

Certainly, many people do give up smoking on the first effort; many also lose the weight they wish to on the first diet program. These are not the people the hypnotist will see; they don't need any assistance. But those who have found the power of the Law of Reversed Effect in their lives may feel utterly incapable of rescuing themselves from it. "I'm a victim of my habit!" becomes an often-heard statement.

Will power is a set of words we nonchalantly toss around when we think someone lacks personal strength. "I can't lose weight because I have no will power," says one woman. She is about fifty pounds over the weight she would like to be. She is also one of the youngest female executives in a large industrial firm. Her income is nearly twice that of her male colleagues; she works up to 16 hours a day; she cares for an invalid mother, supports three charities and spends her "time off" writing novels. No will power? She tearfully described the horrors of "I've got to have that Danish pastry," an impossible-to-fight desire that gets her out of bed an hour early every morning to be first in line for fresh pastry—at the other end of town!

She's got tremendous will power! Nothing stops her in her quest for that Danish, or in her upwardly mobile climb for job success. Will power is not an issue in habit control—to maintain any habit in the face of constant criticism takes amazing will power! If a person had no will power, he couldn't continue a habit . . . it's as though it is will power turned in the wrong direction in that one particular area.

The forced, almost compulsive actions involved for many habituated people may be the consequence of some kind of negative will power. That is, the act of focusing on a problem accentuates and strengthens it. Correspondingly, when that forceful desire to eliminate a habit is removed—replaced with a "who cares?" attitude—the habit will often eliminate itself out of lack of interest or need.

Many become obsessed with their habits, perhaps, through that focusing of will power. This person sees the entire universe colored through the perspective of his habit. "But don't you see?" asked one man in desperation. "I smoke a pack of cigarettes a day—my associates hate it, my wife sends me outside, the kids nag at me all the time! I may lose my job over this . . . and I can't seem to get it off my mind! They follow me everywhere!"

Now we arrive at the meaty part of belief systems, as covered previously in Chapter Two. When your client believes he thinks of nothing but his habit, he has purposely structured his world so that he ignores *any other thoughts*. In fact, he thinks of plenty of other things: driving, getting to work on time, completing an assignment, dressing, eating, communicating with family, etc. By focusing almost exclusively on his habit, he automatically reinforces it! He gives the full power of his attention to it, causing it to thrive. Attention and concentration are potent mental fertilizers.

Indeed, the overweight person is in that condition because he focuses on fatness. Conversely, were he to focus on slimness with as much concentrated effort, he would not be able to stop himself from becoming slim! He diets because he *believes* he is fat, and he is fat because he diets. He wouldn't diet if he didn't believe he was fat; therefore, dieting reinforces overweight! I'm speaking of the person who comes to a hypnotist. He's been on diets and failed, maybe dozens of times. He has "proven" that he can't lose weight, and now he is desperate.

I like to suggest to my clients that they use a modified form of self-hypnosis on a daily basis. I'll ask them to get comfortable during that time, close their eyes, and daydream about themselves *without* the habit. The overweight person imagines himself as slim, the smoker without his cigarette, the nail biter with long nails, the worried person feeling at ease, and so forth. This act of daydreaming, practiced for about five to seven minutes daily, reinforces the desired behaviors, providing a realistic guideline for the unconscious mind. Basically, it takes the focus off the unwanted habit. It's a simple technique that can be surprisingly effective.

The following is a more in-depth view of several popular habit patterns, and how hypnosis can be used to constructively alter them. Keep in mind that I am speaking in general terms and that personal variations do occur.

Overweight

A person is currently considered to be obese if his weight is fifteen per cent over the ideal set by The Metropolitan Life Insurance Company (charts are available in any diet book). Interestingly, those charts are now being challenged by medical research which indicates weight up to *twenty* per cent above the "ideal" may actually be a physical benefit. Such higher weights may help the individual resist disease, but will not contribute to the "dangers" of overweight, such as diabetes, heart difficulties and so forth.

It seems to me that setting arbitrary weight standards is something like defining physical beauty, or defining ideal physical proportions. There is too much diversity between body shapes, use of muscle tissue, density and weight of bone, etc., to make such standards realistic . . . they only work for the hypothetical "average" man or woman. I suggest instead that each client let his or her own body decide what is right and comfortable for it—and not be influenced y advertising which features skeletally thin models. But ıat is a difficult point to get across: "I should weigh 124," ıys one woman. "I feel fine at 135, and look okay, but I on't want to take any chances."

How it happens: Food is a biological necessity. Consum-ıg food is an innate, instinctive action, designed to prolong ıe individual life. Through association and repetition, cer-ıin foods acquire special emotional values: milk-foods are ssociated with early childhood and mother; sweet-foods 'ith rewards and satisfaction; heavy protein-foods with rength and manliness. A person from a particular ethnic roup may have a predilection for foods which have ethnic rigins, due to childhood emotional experiences associated 'ith them.

There are no "good" or "bad" foods—although by talking a confirmed dieter, you might be led to believe that ɔecific foods had committed grievious errors and become ıinted. Carrots are no better than pumpkins or chocolate e cream, or even a big, mushy cream puff, but our dieting iend has assigned emotional values to each of them. Eat-ıg a "bad" food may be associated with being a "bad" erson, or having gone off a diet.

Yet, there are no foods which specifically *cause* over-'eight. An overabundance of any food, including celery alks, can contribute to an overweight condition. The con-ımption of candy or cake may not cause overweight, de-ending on the quantity involved. Millions of Italians eat asta and do not become obese. The Japanese eat tons of ce, but are not known as a fat people.

The overweight person does overeat, consuming more od than can be effectively used by the body, and which then stored as fat. His appetite is hardly a factor, either, nce he will often eat when he's not hungry, and even 'hen he's full. It is acknowledged that the overweight per-ɔn eats to assuage some emotional need—boredom, lone-

liness, sexual frustration, to name a few—each reason a
individual as the person himself. But how did that emo
tional need get associated and confused with hunger, wit
a desire for food?

It's important to note that the average overweight perso
is out of contact with his body systems. For whatever rea
son, he has taught himself not to experience many feel
ings—anger, frustration, energy, sex drive, tiredness
pain—or he may be selective in the feelings he shuts out
for example, only angry "negative" emotions. He con
sciously refuses to deal with the specific feeling, but th
unconscious mind understands and undergoes the reac
tions.

Hunger is an acceptable feeling, necessary for surviva
The overweight person may be constantly hungry, or fee
that sensation instead of any emotions. In other words, h
may feel hungry so he doesn't have to consciously face hi
anger—as if hunger were a legitimate replacement for hi
"negative" feeling. Then, instead of "chewing out the boss,
he can chew up a couple of hamburgers.

To the overweight person, eating is seldom a pleasur
It is instead an emotional act, full of emotional connotation
Even so, most of the connections with food are harsh pro
hibitions—substituting for his prohibitions on specifc fee
ings. He unconsciously resents this, just as anyone woul
protest an undesired jail sentence. It is for this reason th
"dieting" *per se* does not work. Dieting is a physical pun
ishment for an emotional need, something the unconscio
mind does not willingly accept. There may be tempora
success with diets, as the individual asserts some "self-co
trol" or "will power," but that must fade as soon as th
actual emotional issues arise again.

As with most emotional problems, overweight does n
only mean overeating. Fat is a symptom, a sign of som
thing deeper, something so painful that the person simp

cannot deal with it consciously. What could be so frightening?

Symptomatically, excess tissue is a protective layer, a shield against outside disturbance and adversity. The overweight person is protecting himself from facing something hurtful. It may begin with a lack of faith in himself, which expresses itself any number of ways: sexually, in companionship, in sharing, in achievement, in communication skills, in sense of strength. He may even take on a "tough guy" or "bossy" personality to compensate for what he feels he is lacking.

The overweight person deeply and intimately *knows* he cannot meet his own expectations in some specific area. He *knows* he is unworthy of love, or good feelings, or health, or attention, or whatever. He *knows* he is too weak to succeed. He feels tremendously sorry for himself, another feeling he has taught himself to ignore. He is very vulnerable, and knowing that, he has built a wall around himself.

Safe within his physical castle, he is understandably unwilling to give up his carefully constructed protection. But if the walls crumbled around him, he would still be unworthy, still weak and vulnerable—he'd have to develop a new symptom!

Intestinal by-pass operations, stomach stapling, and amphetamines designed to combat overweight mechanically do not work. One client of mine had undergone three intestinal by-passes and resections. She was still overweight, unhappy, bossy, and determined to lose weight. "But, I don't want to hear about any of this emotional stuff," she complained at our first session. "My emotions are just fine. It's my mouth that is the problem." By the following week she had quit our work and had her mouth wired shut. Today, she is still overweight.

The body has its own remarkable resilience; I never

cease to be amazed at what a person can do to himself, and still carry on a seemingly normal life. But I want to emphasize that the body is *not* the problem in overweight. It is the emotions, the habits, and the beliefs which are at fault—and which require the assistance.

The solution: Hypnosis can be the first step to resolving the client's inner confusions that led to becoming overweight. For "typical" overweight people, my work with them might go something like this:

First, I eliminate all words from my vocabulary which connote "loss." "Losing" weight to an overweight person is the equivalent of losing an arm or important body part. "Losing" has negative implications. My clients are "becoming slim and slender," they are *gaining* an improved appearance, not losing parts of themselves. I also avoid the use of berating language with regard to being overweight such as "fat," "tubby" and so forth. The overweight person already has plenty of self-doubt without my help.

Next, we discuss food, diets, and what makes concentration on these worthless. I stress the fact that food is not the problem, but a symptom of a deeper problem that cannot be solved by dieting or restricting behavior. What I'd like to accomplish at this point is give the client enough leeway in his life so he can begin dealing with "good" and "bad" foods as just foods. It's difficult to appreciate the shock and horror "eating anything I want" can bring to the overweight person. Most will express a fear that they will instantly consume everything in sight, gain hundreds of pounds, and mentally disintegrate. What this person does not realize is that as soon as *anything* can be eaten, the pressure to eat forbidden foods disappears—binge behavior eliminates itself when there is nothing that shouldn't be eaten. There's no fun in stuffing yourself on a food that you only wanted because you couldn't have it.

Then, we concentrate on the subject's self-image, how he views himself as an individual. It's at this time that hypnosis is brought into the picture, restructuring the old negative self-image into one more compatible with the desired weight loss.

Eventually, the subject must come to grips with his feelings of inadequacy and be willing to alter his outlook to include a better view of himself emotionally. The ultimate success of the hypnosis will depend on how well this portion of the work is carried out. It's good to keep in mind that it is not usually an overnight process, and most clients will require a good eight weeks or more to accept and put into practice the new beliefs about themselves. I use reframing, age regression, and continual reinforcement of the positive self-image. If the subject has little "slender" behavior to associate with, I will begin developing the "new past" which includes created childhood and adult "thin person" experiences.

As a portion of each session, I will probably also include a little projection work. Having the subject focus on his internal workings and then viewing them from the projected perspective tends to bring him in closer contact with himself. He learns to use internal signals as a worthwhile guide: he feels full and stops eating, senses anger and expresses it, and understands that sexual tension is not relieved by food.

My work is done when the client unconsciously accepts the greater portion of himself, and no longer sees food as the cause of his problem. Weight loss at this point may only have been a few pounds—but the increase in self-esteem and self-reliance should have been great. Most will continue to lose a few pounds each month for up to a year, and then maintain that new weight without effort. This is, of course, because the inner need for extra weight will have been exorcised and replaced with better coping habits.

Occasionally, a subject may return for reinforcement hypnosis. In this situation, he has probably slipped back into old patterns, and only needs his new self-image and behavior reactivated.

Those who complete the process do very well . . . but, unfortunately, not all overweight people really want to solve their difficulty. It is understandably hard to face negative feelings and beliefs about yourself; sometimes it is easier to simply remain overweight and not deal with those thoughts. If the subject fully realizes what will be expected of him before beginning hypnosis—like the woman who had three by-passes and resections—he can make an informed choice of whether he wishes to continue or not. If you are a close watcher of unconscious processes, you'll know before he does which way he'll go.

CHILDBIRTH

There is no natural occurrence which has been treated with as much traditional foolishness as childbirth. What is essentially the outgrowth of abundant good health is largely classed with disease and handled by the medical establishment as though no female could survive without technical interference.

The United States, according to Doris Haire of the International Childbirth Education Association, runs sixteenth behind other developed countries in newborn survival rates. She emphasizes birth practices such as medication, separation of mother from family support, bed confinement, shaving of birth area, induction of labor, chemical stimulation of labor, birth delays to suit hospital schedules, use of anesthesia, routine episiotomy (cutting of vaginal opening to enlarge it), supine position, separation of mother and newborn, and delaying of breast feeding to be at fault in the process.[1]

Childbirth, though one of the most universal, natural processes, is nevertheless regarded as a medical emergency. It is the treatment of birth in this way which makes it more difficult and dangerous than it needs to be. Current practices invite dependency, pain, and prolonged labor simply by ignoring the individual woman's psychological needs for encouragement and helpful support. The use of episiotomies, cesarean section (surgery to remove the baby from the womb through the abdomen), forceps, and medication have resulted in permanent injury to both mother and child.

This is not to say that "abnormal" labor does not occur, or that such situations don't deserve all the professional medical attention required to ease mother and child both. But the vast majority[2] of births are utterly "normal," completely free of any complications which require interference.

Hypnosis, as might be expected, has already been used as anesthesia in childbirth, particularly where the health of mother or child, or both, would be endangered by chemical anesthesias. Further, hypnosis is the basis for all "natural" childbirth systems, from Dick-Read and Bradley through Lamaze,[3] though the particular technique varies. The approach which I have used with my clients and myself is something of a combination of hypnotism, education, and an alteration of expectation from "pain" to "work."

The childbirth process: Childbirth is divided into several identifiable stages, each with distinct physical and psychological components.

The *first stage* consists primarily of labor contractions: the uterus, which has safely housed the baby for about 9 months, begins regular, rhythmic, and gradually stronger muscular contractions which are designed to push the child past the dilating cervix into the birth canal. It is a time of increasing muscular work, which may seem to be happening outside of the woman's control. Left alone, the contractions become stronger and of more consistent duration and can be timed nearly to the second. This stage can last anywhere from one to twenty four hours, though the average is about twelve to fifteen hours.

The *transition stage* occurs as the cervix fully dilates and the baby's head begins its transit into the birth canal. Contractions continue throughout this time, and many women will experience their first legitimate desire to "push," or assist the contractions voluntarily. It is in the transition stage that the woman's emotional levels become most volatile—she may feel irritable, may cry or vomit, or may demand to be made unconscious. The transition stage passes quickly, however, and so does the mood.

The *second stage* encompasses the passage of the baby down the birth canal, with its subsequent intensity of sensation. Internal organs are moved during this stage to make way for the passage of the child; there is a subsequent stretching of the canal, and preparation of the vaginal opening for the imminent birth. It is in the tensing of internal muscles that some women experience discomfort here. The entire process, however, moves slowly enough for all physical systems to accommodate even a very large baby. The second stage is completed with the baby's birth, after about two hours. Some women experience a "birth orgasm" (just as if engaging in a sexual act), which in itself says a great deal about the "pain of childbirth."

The *third stage* is the time when the placenta, or membrane which has provided the baby with nutrients during gestation, is expelled. Contractions continue during this time, or there may be a normal lull in the uterus' action. Expulsion of the placenta is aided by immediate breast feeding, which releases a powerful hormone into the woman's system to begin final contractions. The third stage may last from fifteen minutes to several hours.

The individual woman may experience minor contractions for several days following birth, comparable to menstrual cramps, as the uterus and surrounding tissues resume pre-pregnancy proportions.

Pain: There is nothing so unusual or so bizarre in childbearing that should merit the stories of "incredible pain" which often accompanies it, except perhaps the traditional creator of pain: fear. When a woman is ignorant of her own reactions, when she faces the unknown, when all her training and education have prepared her for the worst, when all she expects is agony, it is only natural for her to be afraid. Imagine that the act of swallowing was given such a lifetime of buildup—the sensations, the movement of food or liquid down the esophagus, the alteration of breathing which occurs. Few would swallow, except when forced by nature or circumstance to do so.

Fear creates an automatic self-protective response. The body prepares itself for the "fight or flight" reaction by sending nutrients and hormones to the muscles. The muscles tense for action. But tension does not encourage ease of movement; it hinders it. A good performer is relaxed on stage—if he is tense, the entire audience will know it by his jerky, uncoordinated movements and delivery. Similarly, a woman in active labor can be fearful enough to create extreme muscular tension—enough tension to undo the work automatically being done by the uterus. It becomes a war of muscle against muscle, which escalates into more fear, tension and pain.

The obvious but seldom used method to combat this syndrome is to eliminate the initiating fear. There is certainly an intensity of experience in childbearing, but intense feeling is not necessarily painful—only when misread. By education about the childbirth process, understanding the physical mechanics involved, and the willingness to experience new and unique bodily awareness, women can undergo childbirth without pain.

The hypnosis for childbirth: I am operating under the assumption that the woman you are working with has already secured medical advice with regards to her pregnancy and childbirth; that you have verified with her doctor or midwife that she has requested hypnosis and that they have no objections; that the decision on where the baby will be born has been made, and all are in agreement; that the type of birth program (i.e., "natural," Lamaze, routine hospital, etc.,) has been decided; and that the woman's close family has no objections to the use of hypnosis.

Having established that much, the hypnosis itself must begin with an education process, a process too complicated to cover here. Recommended reading includes Suzanne Arm's *Immaculate Deception* and *Commonsense Childbirth* by Lester Dessez Hazell, as well as observer-attendance at as many hospital and home births as you can. You will only begin to transmit confidence when you feel sure of the birth process as a natural, uncomplicated act.

In the past, hypnosis has been used as anesthesia in hospital births, but it can be used as a powerful relaxation agent where anesthetic effects are not desired. In either case, your approach is initially the same: developing a deep, comfortable state of hypnosis. For the anesthetic effects, your hypnosis would progress into glove anesthesia, transferable into the abdomen and birth canal. For relaxation, concentrate your efforts on maintaining a hypnotic state in the woman with her eyes open, with her moving about, and with lots of noise and commotion around. In both situations, you will want to "rehearse" the birth itself, going through each stage with the expectation of hypnosis aiding her in whatever way is desired. The rehearsal is important, especially for a first-time mother, to provide an experiential guideline for her inner mind to follow during the process. I also include a suggestion that the woman's breathing will be an appropriate response to the work her body is doing.

I also suggest that you provide self-hypnosis instruction, as outlined briefly at the beginning of the chapter, so that the woman may practice on her own, or if you cannot be present at the birth.

Alcoholism

A person becomes "an alcoholic" when liquor begins to interfere with his life. One woman becomes violent after her first glass of wine; a man goes on a systematic five-day binge every sixty-eight days; another woman drinks a pint of gin mixed with milk every day, as she has done for over fifty years; each calls himself or herself an alcoholic.

Everyone who has ever worked with an avowed alcoholic has a different remedy. Alcoholics Anonymous uses rigorous self-examination and honesty; Transactional Analysis isolates the "crazy child" and alters his behavior[4]; psychotherapy searches for roots in dependency and the symbol of the bottle; medicine supplies drugs which cause vomiting if liquor is ingested, and behavior modification conditions an aversion reaction. All of these systems work—but not for everybody.

It is the same with hypnosis. It works, but not for each person who wants to give up the addiction. There is a fundamental difference between hypnosis and the other remedies, however: I do not see alcohol as the problem. As with the overweight person, alcohol dependence or abuse is a symptom of a deeper difficulty. Like overweight conditions, use of the symptom was chosen sometime in the individual's past to offset a problem—and the subject may not actually want to eliminate that protective barrier.

Typically, the alcoholic has a hard time being rigorously honest with himself. He has developed an elaborate system of rationalizations which allow him to continue his self-deception. AA has been so effective in the past because each of its members is required to drop the veneer and really look under the surface in an atmosphere that encourages honesty.

Again like the overweight person, the alcholic is out of contact with his body: it does not *feel* good to be continuously loaded, anymore than being full all the time feels good. It hurts to have a hangover, to experience nausea and vomiting, to nurse a bruise or broken bone after a fall. Emotionally, it hurts to wake up in a jail cell, be charged in traffic court, or be criticized by family and friends. But, for someone who drinks too much, it might be a worthwhile tradeoff to keep that nasty little something hidden deep in the unconscious.

As far as continued use of alcohol goes, common sense tells us that when the underlying problem is eliminated, the need to drink excessively is also eliminated. In my practice, it has been difficult to ascertain how precise this idea is: most drinkers will choose to stop using liquor entirely, rather than return to moderate or little use. I suspect this is the product of societal training, or possibly the desire to avoid what has seemed to be their downfall in the past.

Our culture has taught that to be "cured" of alcoholism one must avoid liquor altogether. The former drinker may feel a special assurance in being able to say he hasn't had a drink for several years. However, that is something like saying, in roundabout terms, that if he does drink again he's going to be back where he started. He is never really safe from alcohol ever again. That strikes me as being comparable to the formerly overweight person claiming to have been "off" chocolate for years: one slip and the whole fearful process may begin again!

Clients I work with must voluntarily choose to give up alcohol—I do not make it a necessary part of the hypnosis conditioning. It's something of a radical approach, but each subject spontaneously makes that important decision. Generally, this occurs after an obligatory accident or mishap of some sort, where the subject suffers some personal or emotional injury and consequently feels compelled to "get serious" about this approach. I don't know why this happens so consistently. Perhaps continued suggestion that the subject rely on unconscious prompting requires a special signal to set him off in the right direction, something *big* to prove his own ability to cope.

There is a time period following the abstinence from liquor in which the former drinker undergoes a dramatic change of consciousness. His awareness is altered so substantially that he literally becomes another person. Colors may take on extra intensity; he may become especially conscious of other people; he may suddenly recall long and involved dreams. It is as if the influence the alcohol has had on him has kept these inner revelations in check—some researchers have gone so far as to suggest that alcoholism hides psychosis, and the absence of drink allows that aberration to arise. But I suspect that the former drinker must deal with a world he has purposely spent time avoiding . . . a world in which he experiences a direct, belief-level conflict. His beliefs have centered on his inability to cope with this environment without the intervention of liquor; now he must deal with those beliefs as they present themselves, graphically and abruptly. It is the most strenuously difficult part of his work and requires cautious handling.

Using hypnosis: This is a difficult problem to work with hypnotically because the client's conscious and unconscious signals can differ so radically. He may be saying one thing in perfect sincerity, while his unconscious mind indicates the opposite. Trust the unconscious.

I tell each subject that I do not know how long it will take for him to stop his alcohol abuse; that we work at each session with the material his inner mind presents for exploration; that drinking is a symptom of something deeper, and our work will deal with that, not with his handy bottle.

I also indicate that we will not talk about me, except in the most non-personal terms—no tradeoffs of "you have a fault, I have a fault," as can otherwise happen. I've got my eccentricities, but comparison tests between me and my client accomplish nothing. Occasionally, a subject will have an unconscious need to deify or idealize the hypnotist. Perhaps it's a way of projecting his own need for perfection—something that is never quite reached, and produces much guilt. Such a subject may reason that since he is being "picked on" by the hypnotist who points out "flaws," he has a similar right to pick and point. This may also express itself as an exaggerated self-abuse, a kind of "See how awful I am." Neither system works, but contributes instead to the alcoholic condition. Nobody is continuously wonderful or terrible—a fact that is obvious on one level, but entirely missing from another level in the drinker's mind.

Session work, then, is devoted to bringing conscious and unconscious responses in line. This constitutes a definite alteration in consciously accepted ideas, and takes a great deal of time for the client to integrate.

Just about the time the subject has brought most of the

conscious/unconscious signals together, he can be expected to have his obligatory accident, and swear off alcohol entirely.

Now the hard part begins. The subject wonders if he will be able to survive the frightening and sudden changes he is undergoing in consciousness. Hypnosis is directed toward helping integrate and accept these changes. This period can last up to three months, and I do allow the subject to phone me, if it becomes too hard, between sessions. I do this with the stipulation that the client will take the suggestions I offer—not letting him use me as a "patsy."

You must keep in mind that if the client is not willing to make some decisions on his own, he will get nowhere. When I offer my home phone number, it is with the intention of allowing the subject to "touch base" in a frightening moment, not to provide a parent-substitute full of reprimands. I generally suggest that the client go out to a movie, talk to friends, take a walk, and so forth—something to remove him from the surroundings that he may be associating with drinking or his fear. But if he will not take my first or second suggestion, especially if he provides an unnecessary excuse, I will politely inform him that he must make his own decisions, and that I can help no more than he will let me. Then it is only a matter of time: either he will correct his behavior or end the sessions.

After that alteration-of-consciousness period, the subject can usually handle most situations without further hypnosis. I generally do follow-ups every six months.

Nervous Habits

Certain habits, such as nail biting, smoking, facial and muscular tics, excessive talking, stammering, stuttering, and countless other habits have a common root: nervousness. An excess of energy, which requires expression, finds a "home" in some body system—probably not the one it was generated from. A woman smokes because she hates her job but won't give it up; a young man stammers when speaking to strangers because he is worried about his appearance; a girl giggles when dealing with authority figures; all are nervous, tense and uncertain of their own worth.

If nervousness could be drawn, it would probably be shown as a jagged, back and forth line, oscillating rapidly from left to right, from positive to negative. The nervous person rapidly oscillates between emotions such as love and hate, fear and bravery, right and wrong. Middle ground is elusive, and that solidity of belief is threatening in it's own way: what if the middle line is wrong, too? The nervous person is trying to walk a tightrope between the acceptable and non-acceptable, but in his own estimation he is not quite making it.

You cannot permanently relax a nervous person until the variations and discrepancies in his right/wrong system have been dealt with. To do this, the individual client must understand what makes him nervous, if only on an unconscious level. Reframing is an excellent tool here, letting the subject deal with his inner systems in his own way. The "nervous" part is isolated, understood and dismissed to carry on more productive work.

In the few cases where a nervous habit is the result of a particular incident—a muscular tic while driving as the result of an auto accident—age regression is valuable. The event should be revived and repeated until its importance has been eliminated.

Sexual Dysfunction

The reproductive act has been regarded in our society, until very recently, as something of a sacred mystery. The individual's worries, feelings, doubts and fears about sex in general and intercourse in particular could not be expressed, lest he offend or disturb or shock someone. That repressed emotional climate, which is *still* around, has led to a myriad of sexual dysfunctions, which, in large measure, respond very well to hypnotic conditioning.

Conflict, fear and guilt are at the base of most sexual disorders. Reaching these basic motivations is part of the difficulty in the reconditioning of the subject, and may require extensive re-education regarding the sex act itself. False beliefs and fears can cause much damage, and may be held so tenaciously that only intensive psychological counseling may help. Sometimes, encouraging the subject to read simple books on the sex act will correct his faulty outlook. I'll also suggest that the subject wander through "adult marital supply" stores as a means of eliminating unnecessary modesty or guilt.

Impotence: "Impotence" is an all-encompassing term for male sexual inadequacy. It includes, as symptoms of its various aspects, the inability to achieve and/or maintain an erection, premature ejaculation, sexual apathy, anesthesia or pain during climax, and lack of satisfaction during the act.

In the majority of subjects with this complaint, it is caused by psychological factors. Frank Caprio, M.D.[5], has said that impotence is the symptom-consequence of unresolved neurotic conflicts, which is to say, a problem generated by the mind. One client of mine complained of "not being able to enjoy my wife" after a nearly disastrous week-end parachute jump, where his chute had failed to open until the last moment. He was still a little panicky about his close brush with death—which was reflected not only in sexual problems, but in a tepid attitude toward his entire life. Hypnosis aimed toward reestablishing his enjoyment of living proved to be very effective.

Men who suffer from non-organic impotence of long duration will also harbor feelings of inadequacy and a lack of masculinity. Fear of repeated "failure" will be predominant in their thoughts, and may color all their daily activities. Common causes of impotence reactions can include: sexual ignorance, fallacies about masturbation, fear, guilt, disgust, conflicts involving religious or parental censure, masochism or sadism, repressed homosexuality or bisexuality, fear of pregnancy, and familial hostility. There are, of course, any number of possible factors involved with any particular man.

It may even be necessary to use hypnotic conditioning on the man's partner, especially where it becomes apparent that the partner contributes to the man's difficulty. Instructions for patient understanding, avoidance of criticism and the use of encouragement and cooperation should be suggested.

Hypnotic conditioning of the subject will consist of an initial determination of the type of impotence reaction. A client, for example, who feels nothing during climax has an entirely different view of his sexuality than a man who cannot maintain an erection. Regression with insight or reframing should follow, but in every case some education about the nature of human sexuality should be included. Once again, I must refer you to outside reading on this vast subject: anything by Masters and Johnson, or LoPiccolo's *Handbook of Sex Therapy*, will answer virtually any question that should arise. Strangely, impotence is often the result of misinformation concerning masturbation or intercourse.

Frigidity: "Frigidity" is an overall term for sexual inadequacy in the female. It is not always characterized by a lack of desire for sexual contact. It is, as so much of what a hypnotist deals with, a symptom, one which causes the woman difficulty in achieving orgasm during intercourse.

There are a number of different possible causes for frigidity. Among these can be: prudish attitude (which is more common among women than men), fear of damage to her genital organs, fear of pregnancy, resentment toward her partner, lack of understanding from her partner, hostility, narcissism, or male impotence.

Unless the frigidity is the result of pelvic displacement, injury or an illness, it is psychological in origin. Its roots, as with all psychosomatic difficulties, can be traced back to an initiating incident or incidents. It is important to determine when the frigidity first occurred; whether it is consistent with all partners or not, and the subject's attitude toward the sex act.

The causative factor will give you an indication of the type of hypnotic conditioning that will be most successful. A subject, for example, whose first sexual experience was rape by a stepfather will require a more delicate conditioning than a subject who may be using her lack of climax as punishment for her partner.

Be aware of other physical symptoms which may occur along with frigidity. Many women who do not climax satisfactorily also experience intense headaches, backaches, and arm and leg pains. These may be the result of unrelieved sexual tension, or further aspects of the psychosomatic nature of the problem. Pain during the sex act (dyspareunia) and painful menstruation (dysmenorrhea) can also accompany frigidity.

Begin your hypnosis with a history of the problem. For women who have never experienced a climax, it may be necessary to describe the subjective feelings. Determine the subject's attitude toward sex. An important question here is whether or not the subject disrobes in the presence of her partner—excessive modesty can restrict experiencing the full orgasm.

With this subject, I usually recommend regression back to her first sexual encounter, as well as to any occurrences that may still influence her attitudes—especially childhood experimentation and parental training. First intercourse is an emotionally charged occasion, the circumstances of which may color the subject's entire sexual history afterwards. It should be thoroughly desensitized, with insight provided as needed.

It may be necessary—and this may be the case if the subject is ignorant about the sex act or has unusual fears—to provide suitable reading material appropriate to her questions. *The Hite Report* is useful here.

Occasionally, the subject may be frigid with a particular partner, due solely to the partner's inadequate technique or impotence. In this case, the best results can be obtained by conditioning the male partner as well. The only shortcoming to this matter, however, is that a woman who is non-orgasmic for this reason may not realize that her partner is impotent or lacking in technique. Your specific questioning should determine this possibility early in the sessions.

Hypnosis can be used as an adjunct to sex therapy, but please remember that treating a sex problem does not grant sexual license. In most states, there are prohibitions about "sexual contact" with clients, regulations which must be scrupulously adhered to. Generally, you will remain legal—

and ethical—if you do not physically touch or disrobe your clients.

Some Thoughts

A man, desperate by all outwards signs, asked for my assistance in controlling his drinking problem. Just starting out in practice, I eagerly agreed, happy for a chance to use my hypnotic expertise on such a difficult ailment.

Taking a brief history of his situation, it turned out that this man had not only been through AA, behavior modification, and vomit-inducing medication, but was also planning to see a spiritual healer. I had to ask myself, "How is it that this man has had the benefit of all these fine therapies, and still continues to hang on to his symptom?" And being a trusting neophyte, I answered myself that I would be the instrument of his ultimate cure.

Not surprisingly, the man responded extremely well to the hypnosis—just as he had to his previous therapies—and continued to drink heavily, with no hope for discontinuing it in sight. Finally, after three exasperating months, it occurred to me to ask him just what he was trying to prove by *not* altering his problem. It was interesting to see conscious and unconscious processes so in conflict. Sure, he had really put effort into his session; yes, he had done all the exercises I suggested he do on his own; why, then, no progress?

Unconsciously, the man indicated, he was doing precisely what he wanted—proving that no one could help him. Consciously, he couldn't understand. He was doing everything right, wasn't he? Everything but the final step: proving he *could* be helped.

People come to a hypnotist with various habits. They

also come to the hypnotist as a kind of "last resort," having tried many other types of therapies first. This person, therefore, has a history of failing to resolve his problem. This is not a small issue—it's a part of the problem.

Instilling a sense of potential, a possibility of success and expectation, is frequently the most difficult part of this entire situation.

Finally, you cannot work against the intentions of the subject's inner mind, a point I've stressed throughout this book. If your subject is bent on failure, you must confront that part of him which is responsible and reframe it appropriately. If he does not want to make that change, he will not. Accepting failure graciously is as much a part of this business as heralding success.

In summary, every habitual pattern initially develops out of need, but it may continue simply as a habit after that need has been met. Will power plays a small part in the whole business of personal change, generally being directed against conscious goals.

The subject's intimate beliefs about his capacities and self-image are integral to promoting the changes he requests. You may discover that focusing on these beliefs produces better results than a direct assault on the habit, which is only a symptom of a deeper problem.

Notes to Chapter Ten

1 Doris Haire: "The Cultural Warping of Childbirth," (International Childbirth Education Association, 1974).

2 Over 90 per cent, in fact.

3 Each of these "natural" childbirth systems is an outgrowth of early Soviet experimentation in conditioned response. They rely on programmed reactions and breathing technique.

4 Transactional Analysis' *Games Alcoholics Play*, by Claude Steiner, is highly recommended reading.

5 Caprio's *How to Solve Your Sex Problems with Self-Hypnosis* (Wilshire, 1973) filled an important spot in the field, but is now hopelessly outdated.

CHAPTER ELEVEN

Beyond the Body: Extrasensory Perception and Hypnosis

The man in my reclining chair was breathing deeply. His physical relaxation was a visible change from a few moments earlier: he was practicing inducing a self-hypnotic state. I watched with only partial attention, glancing at my watch to note the passage of a half minute. I was waiting for a finger signal to let me know that he was ready for my suggestions.

It was a Friday afternoon and he was the last client of the day. I thought of my plans for the evening . . . a pleasant dinner at a nearby restaurant with my husband, perhaps a drive along the beach, a walk in the sand . . .

My subject, fair haired and light skinned, unaccountably blushed, a deep crimson flush beginning at his neck and travelling into his hairline. Surprised, I interrupted his relaxation, asking, "What's happening?"

"I . . . um . . ." he stammered uncharacteristically, "I'm seeing something . . . strange. It's you . . . um . . . and some man, you know, like together . . . um . . . on the beach . . . I . . . um . . . you know . . ."

I instructed him to continue relaxing, knowing exactly what he meant, and where his embarrassment came from. It wasn't the first time a subject had apparently been a party to my private thoughts—or me to theirs. Did he realize I was thinking about my husband? Or did he think the images were his own creations?

"I felt like a peeping tom," he reported later. "The thoughts just seemed to be there, really caught me off guard. I don't usually blush at my own fantasies."

An informal survey among my colleagues turned up the interesting note that all of them had, at one time or another, experienced a similar effect. One man reported having his client hooked up to a biofeedback machine when it occurred: he was silently appreciating her qualities when the indicator on the machine jumped—and continued to do so each time he repeated the thoughts!

But no one could explain why thoughts could be apparently shared so effortlessly. Was it some kind of remarkable coincidence?

ESP

Extrasensory perception is the catch-all term for quite a few feats which go beyond the usual five senses of touch, sight, taste, smell and hearing. Included under that heading is telepathy (mind-reading), clairvoyance and clairaudiance, precognition (foreknowledge of events), psychokinesis (moving objects at will without touching them), psychometry (reading of an object's "energies"), and a host of others, equally unusual.

Recent research at universities and private laboratories

indicates that *something* is at work, the postulated "sixth sense," or a special psychic ability. Traditional tests, such as those conducted by Duke University in the 1950's, involved dice and cards—having the tested subject attempt to perceive results without having sensory contact. When results surpassed statistical averages, the individual was judged to have some "psychic" skill. Unfortunately, statistical testing did not allow for subjective variations within the individual. A fight with one's spouse before testing may have thrown results far off the subject's peak performance levels, but that would never have been reflected in the statistical tables. The subjective value of psychic experience is highly important. Yet, no real definitions have been arrived at.

There is a large occult underground which encourages and espouses psychic development. For the cost of a good dinner, you can have your fortune read and future predicted by self-proclaimed psychics. Some are notably accurate—and have developed extraordinary reputations aiding law enforcement officials. Some are outright frauds. Some use Tarot cards[1], crystal balls[2], candles or other paraphernalia. Some "get" visual impressions, hear voices, see signs or colors. Some can describe the state of your health by looking at your "aura" or energy field.

Then there are the "regular folks," people who have a sudden inspiration to play the three horse in the fifth race—and win big; or people who think of someone distant just as the phone rings with that someone on the line; or those who worried about Uncle Joe just at the moment he died at the other end of the country.

The field is as vast as the mind's potential, and just as unexplored. Between the charlatans and the traditional scientific community lies a vast untouched field, rich with possibilities. But science, on the whole, won't go near it:

it's difficult to empirically assess. The occultists shy away from anything which questions their faith. Both sides tend to be as rigid and dogmatic as the early Church was about earth being the center of the universe.

The situation, at present, is a standoff. A dedicated few continue to work in the field, criticized by both sides. Barry Taff, Ph.D.[3], a UCLA researcher, specializes in haunted houses and "poltergeists,"[4] or mischievous ghosts, which inhabit them. Taff insists that poltergeists are nothing more exotic than emotionally disturbed adolescents, the ones living in the so-called haunted houses. He indicates that they generate a mental energy of some sort, gaining strength from the teenager's mental instability, and project it outward in great bursts into their surroundings—destructive, noisy outbursts that are sometimes violent. Therapy for the youngster will often eliminate the poltergeist activity, or the child may outgrow the phenomena. Sometimes the "ghosts" will simply disappear by themselves.

The question then becomes: what kind of energy is this? The answer is disarmingly simple: no one knows. No sophisticated apparatus has yet been devised to measure the type or quantity of energy involved in psychic displays. Even individuals with publicly acknowledged psychic skills often don't know "where" their talent stems from. Emotional content seems to be important, though. It appears to be easier to "pick up" emotionally charged material. "I just *know*," said one woman shrugging.

That *knowingness* is often the one factor that frightens people at their first taste of psychic awareness. A lifetime of training has taught us to believe that no one can know anything that does not come through his five senses. Therefore, obtaining some piece of information through "other" means (such as dreams, intuition, or just "knowing") is a contradiction of very basic beliefs. That casts a fearful instability on everything believed to be true; it's easier to rationalize or ignore psychic twinges.

But that knowingness persists in many individuals who wish to increase or develop the skill. Hypnosis, and the allied relaxed states, can contribute to this enhancement. There are personal limits of belief, however, past which the subject will not allow himself to go, as you'll see later in the chapter.

COINCIDENCE?

Carl Jung, the famous psychologist, surmised that there were certain recognizable similarities in psychic occurrences, often labeled "coincidences." He published a paper late in his career, in 1952, in an attempt to organize what he felt was a vast and largely ignored field. He believed that "coincidence" which was meaningful to the observer could no longer be considered simple coincidence. He called the "meaningful coincidence" a *synchronistic* event, and the link between two events connected by their meaning *synchronicity*.[5]

Synchronicity requires a viewer or participant because it is an experience in which the individual ascribes meaning to the coincidence. This is not to say that "synchronicity" is the same as "synchronous" occurrences: jets take off and land in synchronous patterns, the movement of traffic may be synchronous, but the meaningfulness of the events is not supported by an individual participant. Often, synchronistic events are accompanied by an emotional response—awe, chills, elation, contentment—as the participant grasps the fullness of the "remarkable coincidence."

Jung described three types of synchronicity:

1. a coincidental relationship between an individual's inner thoughts or feeling and an external event.
2. an individual knowledge, such as a vision or a dream, of an event taking place elsewhere that is later verified.
3. an individual premonition of some occurrence which later happens as it was perceived.

Within those three types of events lies the bulk of psychic experience today, particularly that outside of dogmatic structures. A dream which later "comes true" would fit into the third category, for example. The second category would include "knowing" who was calling on the phone before you answer it.

The first type of synchronicity is a little more difficult to describe, and can best be illustrated by example: I was driving to my office, traversing Los Angeles' vast freeway system, thinking about a difficult client I was to see that day. I was at a loss as to the next step in her sessions. As I drove on, I glanced idly at passing cars' license plates. To my surprise, it was as if the licenses of different cars were giving me an important message: "SEE" on one, "HER" on another, and later, "NEW" on a third. The meaningful coincidence of spotting these license plates at that time sent my mind onto another track entirely, and I was able to resolve the next step in the woman's sessions.

There must have been five hundred other people on the freeway that morning, seeing the same licenses as I did, but for them the event was not synchronistic. It was for me, though, as participant. While this example may not seem significant in the writing, at the time it was highly important and relevant.

Most people can count among their experiences at least one example of synchronicity, a coincidence with meaning.

If we let Jung's three categories provide our definition, then we have a system for determining the basic nature of "psychic" experience. For purposes of simplicity, I'll give each category a general title: the first type of synchronicity will henceforth be "meaningful coincidence;" the second type, an example of "clairvoyance"; and the third type, "precognition."

Hypnosis and ESP

The deeply relaxed state of hypnosis is conducive to the development of synchronistic occurrences. Whether it is because there are fewer conscious "blocks," or because in hypnosis there is "some other" level of mind at work, is open to exploration. Many reputable psychics spontaneously develop hypnotic-like trances when using their skills, among them Edgar Cayce[6], whose first psychic experiences began after being hypnotized several times. For most, however, simply being hypnotized does little to enhance psychic development. As with other hypnotic phenomena, motivation appears to be an important factor.

Motivation, though, usually has an end point. A man who wishes to stop smoking knows his goal. Someone who wishes to develop a photographic memory understands exactly what completion of that means. But when using hypnotism to increase psychic skills, it is a very individual matter as to how far that development can proceed.

My work has indicated that each person will reach a plateau beyond which he will not progress. It is not that he cannot go further, but rather that some part of his mind chooses not to. Since "fear" is often the feeling that lies beyond the plateau, it is reasonable to assume that the individual has reached the upper end of his "psychic belief system"; that is, "I can do this much and no more in safety." Behind such a belief might be religious or scientific training, or limits imposed by parental injunction or society. Sometimes, by allowing the subject a few months—or years—to get accustomed to his skills, he will prepare himself to continue development.

Dr. Taff, who has also been conducting a weekly clairvoyance-development workshop for nearly a decade, has found similar results with his group. There is a hard core of a half-dozen regulars, and probably several thousand others over the years have come and gone. Many people can be frightened by the intensity of psychic awareness, especially when it goes beyond their expectations.

Coming to a definition of success in psychic development using hypnosis, then, becomes the first and most important step. Following that must be a realistic expectation of results. Not everyone is prepared for the personal changes which take place with psychic skills. It's something like owning an old, valuable painting: the emotional value of ownership may or may not balance off the trouble of storing it properly, insuring it, and caring for such a treasure. Similarly, having an unusual psychic skill requires a trade-off of a personal sort for each person who wants it. That trade-off may be only of time, or it may be a major reorganization of life values.

Meaningful coincidence: Author Jane Roberts' experience described in Chapter Six of this book—the synchronicity between the flock of birds she was watching and a symphony playing on the radio—is an excellent example of what occurs with a meaningful coincidence. For any observer, that scene might have had no meaning whatsoever, but the presence of Ms. Roberts as participant changed the event into something with personal significance.

The discovery of meaningful coincidences in one's life is a major step toward the acceptance of further psychic phenomena. It seems to produce a slightly altered focus of awareness and the individual realizes that there is more to his life than surface appearances.

Consequently, when a subject wishes to develop his psychic skills, I will usually begin with his meaningful coincidences, suggesting that he become more conscious of them. Most subjects will report a subtle alteration of their awareness, which they find difficult to define. One woman artist described it as "seeing through the canvas, or the first layers of paint, down to the in-between space where everything is clear." Others have said that they sense a greater continuity to the universe, that things are connected by a gridwork of "meanings." It is admittedly a problem to use objective language to describe subjective experiences.

Clairvoyance: This aspect of psychic ability concerns the awareness of events, happening at a distance from the person, which can be later confirmed. Under this general heading are a series of subcategories which are clairvoyant in nature, but use slightly different approaches: telepathy, psychometry, card reading, and so forth. These variations of clairvoyance seem to be individual eccentricities. The psychometrist, or object-reader, who must hold a person's ring, watch, keys, etc., to perform psychically, is probably using the item as a focal point for his own unconscious mind. There is nothing wrong with it, of course, so I like to encourage the subject to experiment with various approaches until he finds the one that "feels" best.

Clairvoyance can be enhanced by first determining what the purpose of the psychic awareness will be. The subject is asked, then, what he wants to use it for. As with any motivation, your judgment of whether the purpose is a reasonable one or not is unimportant.

If the subject has had a clairvoyant experience previously, so much the better: there is something familiar to draw on, or recreate. Otherwise, the subject will have to form his own system of definitions for psychic occurrences. A deep self-trust must be a part of this, for the individual will have to rely entirely on his hunches and feelings. This reliance will also increase as the subject finds himself getting the right information more often than not. But it is a very big step.

With the subject in hypnosis, I suggest that he focus on some person or object, then allow his mind to "go blank." There is, in fact, no totally empty state of mind, but "going blank" sets up the expectation that something will happen. Some hypnotists effectively use imagery here, having the subject envision a giant movie screen and await pictures, or listen for voices. Again, it is an individual preference, perhaps allied with an individual's representational systems.

Next, the client is asked to let whatever is "there" come into consciousness. Often, on the first few experiences, the subject's reports are virtually meaningless, or at least seem to have little connection with the person or object focused on. Doing this right is as much a matter of practice as learning how to roller skate: in the beginning, the student falls a lot, but shows a slow and steady progress.

I might point out here that the subject many times will have difficulty putting a concept into words. For example, one psychic[7] tried to describe a roof and ceiling, without knowing exactly what she was trying to say. She called it heavy, overhanging, dark—all terms which could be applied to the topic, but not as specific as desired. You can expect this with most subjects initially, but they should become more precise as their skill grows.

The subject's direction of progress will depend upon his

daily interests. If he is fond of animals, he will probably become skilled at "picking up" details about family pets and their habits. If he is concerned about health, the subject will probably begin to register "flashes" about the physical condition of other people, sensing bodily disturbances and illnesses.

Unless you intend to use statistical results of each client's progress as part of a study, I would advise that you ignore the subject's "misses" and concentrate on his "hits." In this way, you will reinforce the positive aspects of what is happening, thereby encouraging him to test and use his ability. He may have one hit out of fifty tries, but that one hit has more potential benefit than any review of misses would. As a positive reinforcement, you might consider having the subject keep a daily record of his hits so that he has a sign of his own progress.

Finally, if something should occur for which you have no explanation, don't be nervous about admitting it. The entire field of ESP is in its infancy. Nobody can answer all the questions.

Precognition: As with clairvoyance, there is a great deal of personal variation in this. One person is concerned with disasters, and dreams in advance about ships sinking; another is interested in her family's welfare and "has a feeling" about the direction of each member's health. Again, the individual should be encouraged to progress in whatever direction his talents lie.

However, accurate precognition does not only depend on personal skill. There seems to be some individual awareness of "probabilities" underlying this branch of ESP. We can imagine any event as the intersection of probabilities. For example, if you step directly in front of a speeding truck, there is a probability of your being struck by it. If we trace that event backward from the perspective of the participants (you and the truck), we might find you an hour earlier coming from a restaurant with the intention of taking a walk. An hour before the probable meeting, that truck might be fifty miles outside the city on its daily run. At that point, one hour before the probable accident, there is a distinctly smaller probability of the incident occurring. You could take a different pathway; the truck could have a flat tire and be held up. Even with the passage of minutes, the probability of the truck and you meeting does not increase appreciably—it is only at the point where you step directly in front of the truck that the probability reaches its zenith.

In similar fashion, precognition becomes a tricky business: the vast number of alternate probable "routes" that any event can take makes knowing the outcome beforehand nearly miraculous. This may also account for the failures of some psychics who concentrate on precognitive material: they may be picking up a probability which simply does not pan out.

For those who wish to explore this branch of ESP, there are several hypnotic routes, depending on the nature of the precognition desired. One of these is through "age progression," the opposite of age regression. With this, the subject is hypnotized and asked to move forward in time, stopping and recounting "something important" happening. Again, personal variations abound. This is also a type of hypnosis fraught with fantasy material, so don't take everything literally. There is one hypnotist who claims to have progressed thousands of people—who all foresee a turn-of-the-century atomic World War III. Sadly, this man also tells each subject details about other people's progressions beforehand, effectively preconditioning each client to come up with the same material. In any case, that probable event is still far enough away for the world to do a great deal to alter its probability.

Another method involves having the subject focus on the situation or person which he wishes to gain precognitive information about, then to await that sense of knowingness to mark his intuitions. Because long range precognition is difficult to check, I advise that the beginning subject concentrate on awareness of daily events, perhaps keeping an early morning journal of "Today's Predictions." It is easy to check, and gives rapid feedback.

Precognitive material may come in dreams, or clothed in symbolic garb. One man dreamed of human bodies falling from the sky, shredding gruesomely in mid-air. He was very upset by the dream because of its vividness, and because he was not prone to such ghoulish nightime activities. Three days later a major air disaster occurred, where a jet did, in fact, break up in the air and spew bodies through the sky.

With that man, we ended up questioning the nature of precognition and clairvoyance—he had known no one on the flight, had flown only twice in his life, had no interest in aircraft—and couldn't find any relationship between himself and the event. We theorized that he had, for some unknown reason, touched on the probability of the accident.

One researcher, biologist Lyall Watson, Ph.D.[8], describes time as a pond. An event like the air disaster might be compared to a pebble dropped into the pond, sending out ripples in all directions, both forward and backward from its position in time. A perceptive person might then be able to sense the ripples as he "nears" the event in time.

Or such an incident might be simply a case of precognitive telepathy—someone scheduled for the plane flight picked up the probability of accident, and "sent out" that message to whatever "receivers" were available. The only difficulty with this possible explanation is that we may never know how many other people picked up the same information.

"But what good does it do?" the man finally asked. "I couldn't do anything about it . . . couldn't help a single one of those people . . . didn't even know if it was going to really happen or not!" Again, this is a matter of personal interpretation, I'm sure. What the man may have needed most at that time was a confirmation that he actually could precognate. He certainly picked a dramatic event: it couldn't be overlooked!

MUTUAL HYPNOSIS

When person A hypnotizes person B, who then hypnotizes person A at the same time, mutual hypnosis is in progress. Two (or more) people are hypnotized by each other, with a specific purpose designated prior to the first induction.

According to theory, since hypnosis does seem to activate ESP levels of mind, two people in mutual hypnosis should be in close mental contact, or at least closer mental contact than usual.

In actuality, there is a typical learning pattern involved. Unless both people are already psychic, they go through the same trial and error processes of development. But mutual hypnosis has demonstrated a speed and efficiency that is difficult to beat. Apparently, when the two minds involved are in agreement, an "opening" or "channel" occurs through which information can pass relatively easily.

A husband and wife interested in psychic development requested mutual hypnosis. I acted as a guide and was not to become involved in their state, only to monitor it. Both were taught hypnosis. In their early sessions, they would hypnotize each other at the same time, then take turns describing "this long path that we walk together." After a half dozen sessions both were able to anticipate the other's suggestions and directions, and could carry on a mental, rather than verbal, conversation. Understandably, such contact required quite a few changes in their personal attitudes, especially ideas about mental "privacy."

The applications of mutual hypnosis are, once again, topics which have hardly been scratched. As with much of psychic development, it's difficult to set precise standards and goals, as well as evaluate results. If one mind, for example, can produce the answer to a math problem in five minutes, would two minds in mutual hypnosis be able to find the answer more quickly? If so, what about ten minds working on the same problem? And to carry that idea a step further, suppose ten minds—or a hundred—all concentrated on one idea, say, creating rain. Would that combined mental energy be enough to influence the environment?[9]

If that worked, we would be in a remarkable position as far as evaluating our beliefs about reality. Could the tremendous mental energy unleashed by thousands of people simultaneously watching a movie like *Earthquake* possibly be sufficient to alter the planet's earthquake patterns? Would a *Jaws* movie set off shark attacks? Or a *Poseidon Adventure* result in ships upending at sea? Or a *China Syndrome* cause a nuclear accident? Or would such a possible relationship between movie and actuality simply be a remarkable coincidence?

Psychic vs. Crazy

One man says he hears voices talking to him all the time. He is in a state mental institution. A woman who hears similar voices is a respected California psychic, with a lucrative practice. Who's the sick one?

Who can tell? All we know is that the man does not fit in with society; the woman does, because she uses her "state of mind" productively.

The concept of productivity is the essence of successful psychic development. It may be wonderful fun, for example, to have an artistic talent, but when that skill cannot be used it turns inward on itself. Talents, as mentioned in Chapter Three, require usage. Using a skill develops it. A psychic talent is worthwhile only if it can be used, just like any other skill. But more than other abilities, it can easily be confused with madness.

Certainly, insanity of different varieties include psychic-type manifestations: hearing voices, seeing visions, meaningful coincidences, knowingness of future events (whether they occur or not), telepathy, etc. But craziness does not have a productive component for the mad individual; it only removes him from unpleasant circumstances. Psychic skills, on the other hand, do have a worthwhile use, even if that value is strictly self-serving.

Except in well-advanced cases, it may be difficult to establish if the client *is* crazy or just psychically gifted. The only way I've been able to find is in unconscious/conscious responses. The person suffering from mental illness sends a barrage of conflicting messages; the psychic tends to have the usual complement of agreeing and conflicting signals. Psychically talented people may be eccentric, but they are not mad.

In summary, there is a certain knowingness which accompanies intuitive awareness, one which reaches into the heart of coincidence and synchronistic events. Results, however, are difficult to assess empirically, and in the past individual subjective variations have not been taken into consideration.

In developing psychic skills, hypnosis may be employed in many ways. It has shown itself to be effective, perhaps because it creates a conducive state of mind. The client must establish his own goals and directions, even though he may find it difficult to progress beyond specific points.

Psychic talents may resemble mental aberrations in some, but while the gifted person may be considered odd, he is not ill.

NOTES TO CHAPTER ELEVEN

1 Tarot cards are an ancient system of 78 cards used for the purposes of divination. Our modern poker deck is derived from the "Minor Arcana" (lesser mysteries) of the Tarot deck.

2 Crystal balls, like the Tarot deck, have an origin in the dim past. The crystal gazer, or scryer, sees images in the ball, which he interprets. Today, a four-inch, quartz-crystal ball of good quality—that is, having no blemishes or imperfections—may fetch up to $1,000.

3 Barry Taff, Ph.D., was an associate of Dr. Thelma Moss, a giant in the field of parapsychology. Besides carrying on his exploration of "haunted houses," he has made numerous TV and radio appearances, written various papers, spoken to many professional groups, as well as served as one of the protagonists in Frank de Fellitta's *The Entity*. The novel is based on one encounter Taff and his associate Kerry Gaynor had with a bizarre poltergeist manifestation.

4 Poltergeists are discussed at length in William G. Roll's *The Poltergeist* (New American Library, 1972).

5 *The Tao of Psychology: Synchronicity and the Self*, by Jean Shinoda Bolen, M.D., (Harper & Row, 1979) is a complete analysis of Jung's synchronicity.

6 Edgar Cayce suffered a psychosomatic throat constriction which interfered with his work as a salesman. Al Layne, a travelling hypnotist, was called in to do what he could for

the afflicted Cayce. Cayce spontaneously developed his own "trances" afterwards, and continued for the next three decades as one of America's top psychics.

7 Jane Roberts, again.

8 In his book, *Gifts of Unknown Things*, (Simon and Schuster, 1977).

9 Jeffrey Goodman, Ph. D., insists it is in his *We Are the Earthquake Generation*, (Berkley Publishing Corp., 1979).

CHAPTER TWELVE

Some Final Thoughts

In 1958, hypnosis was recognized by the American Medical Association as a viable tool and was recommended to its members. By 1978, you could count on one hand the medical schools at which hypnotism was actively being taught. Most psychologists still come to hypnosis via Freud—who didn't like it and wasn't good at it. People who practice hypnosis get strange looks: I've been told that what I really do with my clients is "unspeakably evil witchcraft."

The problem is that most people don't understand hypnosis—not even many of those who *do* it. I don't know what makes the subject's mind accept a suggestion. I only know when it happens. The mystic might say, "When the student is ready, the teacher will be there," and let it go, presupposing an order and dignity to the universe that most Westerners would not accept. This leaves us grasping at the flimsiest "scientific" evidences for our definitions: eyeball rolls, alpha waves and skin resistance.

The old medicine-man is gone, lost from the once sacred places. Instead we have enthroned the "man in white," our scientist. They have their sacred places, too. The sparkling rooms of glass and chrome, with the secret languages and mighty codes on chalkboards, describing the knowledge and power to do the impossible. But something is missing, a subtle, small something that our revered investigators lack—intuition.

In minds trained since infancy to value the tangible, define the seeable, measure the weighable, there has been no place reserved for intuition. The medicine man was intuition's silent partner, trusting in the innate wisdom of his cells to guide his judgments. We have all but forgotten, in our mad labor to objectify everything, that we are made of the same stuff as the planet, the same as trees and snails and concrete. And so we ignore our intuitions.

Hard core objectifiers don't trust hypnosis. "How can you possibly trust something you don't understand?" they reason—and it is good reasoning. After all, how can you trust that the sun will rise in the morning if you don't understand planetary rotation? Can you be certain of anything which cannot be repeated *ad nauseum* in a clinical setting?

The old medicine man was a powerful character. He *knew* things, sometimes without really knowing them. He was the object of hushed speech and questioning looks. If he had the power to heal, perhaps he also had the power to destroy. With a glance, the evil eye could be bestowed.

Today, we hypnotists have cornered the evil eye, but in our civilized world, most people don't really believe that hocus-pocus. The titters of nervous laughter, the half-jokes about eye-contact, the stubborn refusals to experience hypnotic induction, may cover that deeper, instinctive distrust—and admiration—the medicine man once engendered.

Could the hypnotist be the new medicine man?

But Is It Legal?

Having come all the way up from magnetism, passed Freud unscathed and survived sensationalized stage performances to the current day, hypnosis has another great battle ahead. This time, it is with the law.

If you live in Florida, New York or Kentucky, you cannot practice hypnosis as of this writing unless you are also a licensed physician or psychologist. Each year, in state assemblies and senates, new bills are introduced to limit and control the practice of hypnosis.

Many California cities—including Los Angeles, where I practice—have "witchcraft laws." These local regulations make doing palmistry, necromancy, fortune telling, crystal gazing, witchcraft and a host of other "occult sciences" a misdemeanor. Hypnosis, interestingly, is included in that listing of misdemeanor activities. Fortunately, it is not now being enforced in L.A.—but it *is* enforced in some other counties, as far as hypnotists go.

Sadly, the whole question of "Who is skilled enough to be legally allowed to perform hypnosis?" ignores several vital factors which make the question almost meaningless.

Those who keep asking who shall be allowed to hypnotize have forgotten—if they ever knew—that no one is hypnotized without his consent, whether that hypnosis is formal or informal. Beneath this is that most popular misconception: that he who uses hypnosis has some innate power or ability to influence, to *make* others do what he or she wants. I can't tell you how many times I've tried to get someone to rob a bank for me, do away with the landlord or steal a car. My efforts are always doomed to failure!

Furthermore, where does the hypnosis end and other disciplines take over? Television commercials are probably some of the most carefully designed, intelligently conceived, hypnotic suggestions of our time. Is there anything worse than "houseitosis" or, heaven forbid, body odor? I've caught myself humming the catchy themes for a major brand of soda pop, just as my hand (all by itself, no doubt) took a bottle of it off the supermarket shelf.

Subliminal advertising[1], that covert shot at the unconscious mind, is literally everywhere—billboards, magazines, television, radio, even in movies. Though it uses the same mechanisms of mind as hypnosis, designed to be absorbed by the unconscious without conscious interference, is it not hypnosis because it uses a different title?

"Natural" childbirth, with its rigorous relaxation exercises, controlled breathing techniques and basis in Pavlovian conditioned responses, is nothing more than unadulterated self-hypnosis. Dianetics, est, Silva, TM, Biofeedback and the other programs mentioned in Chapter One, are all varieties of hypnotic phenomena.

Who is skilled enough to legally perform hypnosis? Apparently, legislators believe that advertisers, childbirth coaches, students of TM or est, commercials and billboards are—but not hypnotists. It's doubly unfortunate that intelligent people who have received M.D.'s or Ph.D.'s from their respective states aren't necessarily going to be good hypnotists: the addition of a degree does not confer hypnotic skills. Hypnotism is seldom taught in medical schools, but is primarily carried on by private individuals.

The problem, once again, is the definition of hypnosis, what it can do, and what it cannot. The right of self-responsibility and self-determination has been neglected. It is the duty of each hypnotist to inform, and to correct mistaken notions. Only by a sustained effort to educate can hypnosis survive and flourish into the next century.

Notes to Chapter Twelve

1 Subliminal advertising received its best recounting from Wilson Bryan Key in his *Subliminal Seduction, Ad Media's Manipulation of a Not So Innocent America*, (New American Library, 1974).

APPENDIX ONE

Conducting Sessions

Ingredients: one hypnotist, one subject, one quiet, comfortable location.

1. *Getting clients:* Volunteers for practice work are easy; paying clients come from advertising and referrals. Local directory ads (Yellow Pages) have a good track record, as well as small local papers. Large metropolitan papers seem to provide less returns per cost, perhaps because ads get lost among the thousands of others. University papers always get excellent results, although the clients are usually financially limited.

2. *Making an agreement:* Each client should fully clarify what he wishes to work on—and you must likewise specify exactly what you will do for him. Without a sound agreement, there is room for confusion and disillusionment to grow. Write it down, and keep it on file.

3. *First session:* As well as making the agreement on what is to be done, you will wish to establish the subject's history, previous hypnosis experiences, and the medical/

legal ramifications of your work together. In many states, for problems dealing with physical health, you are required to obtain a referral from a physician before beginning to work with a client. Be sure to explain your fee schedule, and determine whether the client will pay on a session-by-session basis, or be billed monthly for your services.

4. *Following sessions:* Keep a written record of the work you have done at each session—just a note will do, as long as it can act as a reminder. You will probably spend each session this way: 20 minutes of discussion and determination of work to be done; 20 minutes of hypnosis; 15 minutes of planning work the subject is to do for the week.

5. *The unexpected:* Interruptions from ringing phones, people entering unexpectedly (salesmen are the worst offenders), earthquakes, blown fuses, and so forth *do* happen, but not too often. If your client is in hypnosis, keep your voice calm, and handle the problem as quickly as possible.

6. *Concluding your work:* When a client has accomplished what he came for, or has indicated that he has no intention of keeping his part of the agreement made at your first session, your work together is finished. I promise each client that I will keep in contact, then I'm careful to do a follow-up every six weeks or so. Some clients do become my friends after a time, and for these I keep hypnosis and friendship separate. Remember that any files or records you have kept are not, by law, confidential. If there is anything in a client's records that might compromise him, you should destroy it.

APPENDIX TWO

Suggested Reading

There is no speedier way to become a poor hypnotist than to read just one book, or take just one course, and assume that you thoroughly understand the subject. Because the limits of hypnosis are the ones you personally impose, the more you know—about everything—the better a hypnotist you will become.

This suggested reading list is a compilation of books which, I believe, are indispensable for developing hypnotic skills through greater knowledge. Some of the included texts are technical works, some are for the interested amateur, some are not strictly about hypnosis at all. But each book offers an important contribution to the hypnotist's *mind*, and will help make your use of hypnosis a constructive, positive act.

Arieti, Silvano, *The Interpretation of Schizophrenia* (Basic Books, 1974). This classic in the field of psychotherapy is a useful guide to mental illness.

Bandler and Grinder, *Frogs into Princes, Neuro Linguistic Programming* (Real People Press, 1979). Their refreshingly informal discussions are loaded with useful insights.

Cooke and Van Vogt, *Hypnotism Handbook* (Borden, 1965). An old stand-by with useful formats.

Fromm and Shor, *Hypnosis: Developments in Research and New Perspectives* (Aldine Publishing, 1979). A comprehensive listing of current studies and possibilities.

Furst, Arnold, *Post-Hypnotic Instructions* (Wilshire Book Co., 1969). This little gem provides a useful, if sometimes dated, outline of suggestions for various problems.

Garfield, Patricia, Ph.D., *Creative Dreaming*, (Simon and Schuster, 1974). Dreams are a mirror of unconscious activity. This book provides insights on how to use that to good advantage.

Haley, Jay (Ed.), *Advanced Techniques of Hypnosis and Therapy, Selected Papers of Milton H. Erickson, M.D.* (Grune and Stratton, 1967). Erickson's work a la Erickson. Invaluable.

Hubbard, L. Ron, *Dianetics* (Church of Scientology, 1950). He doesn't say anything new, but it is the way he puts it . . .

LeCron, Leslie, *Self-Hypnotism* (New American Library, 1964). A hypnosis classic.

Kroger and Fezler, *Hypnosis and Behavior Modification: Imagery Conditioning* (Lippincott, 1976). Mostly good visualization techniques, some of it silly.

Lowen, Alexander, M.D., *The Betrayal of the Body* (Macmillan Publishing, 1978). Delightfully sane interpretation of the results of a lack of bodily awareness.

Perls, Frederick, M.D., Ph.D., *Gestalt Therapy Verbatim* (Bantam Books, 1972). Hard core common sense.

Roberts, Jane, *The Nature of Personal Reality, A Seth Book* (Prentice-Hall, 1974). Has some remarkable insights into "natural hypnosis," and self-responsibility.

Rossi, Ernest and Sheila, and Erickson, Milton, *Hypnotic Realities* (Irvington, 1976). A bit dry, but an excellent guide.

Spiegel and Spiegel, *Trance and Treatment, Clinical Uses of Hypnosis* (Basic Books, 1978). Full of useful theory.

Steiner, Claude, *Scripts People Live* (Bantam, 1975). A self-responsibility guidebook, and an eye-opener.

Tart, Charles T., (Ed.), *Altered States of Consciousness* (Doubleday Anchor, 1969). Hypnosis to dreams to drug use, an indispensable guide.

Index